T0189296

PARALLEL, OBJECT-ORIENTED, AND ACTIVE KNOWLEDGE BASE SYSTEMS

The Kluwer International Series on
ADVANCES IN DATABASE SYSTEMS

Series Editor
Ahmed K. Elmagarmid

Purdue University
West Lafayette, IN 47907

Other books in the Series:

DATABASE CONCURRENCY CONTROL: Methods, Performance, and Analysis
by Alexander Thomasian
     ISBN: 0-7923-9741-X
TIME-CONSTRAINED TRANSACTION MANAGEMENT: Real-Time Constraints in
Database Transaction Systems
by Nandit R. Soparkar, Henry F. Korth, Abraham Silberschatz
     ISBN: 0-7923-9752-5
SEARCHING MULTIMEDIA DATABASES BY CONTENT
by Christos Faloutsos
     ISBN: 0-7923-9777-0
REPLICATION TECHNIQUES IN DISTRIBUTED SYSTEMS
by Abdelsalam A. Helal, Abdelsalam A. Heddaya, Bharat B. Bhargava
     ISBN: 0-7923-9800-9
VIDEO DATABASE SYSTEMS: Issues, Products, and Applications
by Ahmed K. Elmagarmid, Haitao Jiang, Abdelsalam A. Helal, Anupam Joshi, Magdy Ahmed
     ISBN: 0-7923-9872-6
DATABASE ISSUES IN GEOGRAPHIC INFORMATION SYSTEMS
by Nabil R. Adam and Aryya Gangopadhyay
     ISBN: 0-7923-9924-2
INDEX DATA STRUCTURES IN OBJECT-ORIENTED DATABASES
by Thomas A. Mueck and Martin L. Polaschek
     ISBN: 0-7923-9971-4
INDEXING TECHNIQUES FOR ADVANCED DATABASE SYSTEMS
*by Elisa Bertino, Beng Chin Ooi, Ron Sacks-Davis, Kian-Lee Tan, Justin Zobel, Boris Shidlovsky
and Barbara Catania*
     ISBN: 0-7923-9985-4
MINING VERY LARGE DATABASES WITH PARALLEL PROCESSING
by Alex A. Freitas and Simon H. Lavington
     ISBN: 0-7923-8048-7
DATA MANAGEMENT FOR MOBILE COMPUTING
by Evaggelia Pitoura and George Samaras
     ISBN: 0-7923-8053-3

PARALLEL, OBJECT-ORIENTED, AND ACTIVE KNOWLEDGE BASE SYSTEMS

by

Ioannis Vlahavas

and

Nick Bassiliades

Department of Informatics
Aristotle University of Thessaloniki
Greece

KLUWER ACADEMIC PUBLISHERS
Boston / Dordrecht / London

Distributors for North America:
Kluwer Academic Publishers
101 Philip Drive
Assinippi Park
Norwell, Massachusetts 02061 USA

Distributors for all other countries:
Kluwer Academic Publishers Group
Distribution Centre
Post Office Box 322
3300 AH Dordrecht, THE NETHERLANDS

Library of Congress Cataloging-in-Publication Data

A C.I.P. Catalogue record for this book is available
from the Library of Congress.

*The publisher offers discounts on this book when ordered in bulk quantities. For
more information contact: Sales Department, Kluwer Academic Publishers,
101 Philip Drive, Assinippi Park, Norwell, MA 02061*

Printed on acid-free paper.

Printed in the United States of America

To my wife Chrysoula and my daughters Iro and Danae

Ioannis Vlahavas

To my fiancée Evdokia and my parents

Nick Bassiliades

Contents

List of Figures/Tables   ix

Foreword   xi

Preface   xiii

1. INTRODUCTION   1

Basic Terminology   5

PART I. KNOWLEDGE BASE SYSTEMS   11

2. DEDUCTIVE AND ACTIVE DATABASES   13

Introduction: The Rule Spectrum   13

Deductive Databases   15

Active Databases   20

3. INTEGRATION OF MULTIPLE RULE TYPES   27

Unification of Production and Deductive Rule Semantics   27

Integration of ECA Rules in Declarative Rule Conditions   28

Integration of Declarative Rules in Active Databases   30

4. AN ACTIVE OBJECT-ORIENTED KNOWLEDGE BASE SYSTEM   37

The System Architecture   37

The Rule Language   39

Integration of Declarative Rules   41

Condition Compilation and Matching   46

Optimization and Extensibility   54

PART II. PARALLEL DATABASE AND KNOWLEDGE BASE
          SYSTEMS   61

5. PARALLEL DATABASE SYSTEMS   63

Introduction   63

Parallel Query Execution   65

Parallel Database System Architectures   71

Data Partitioning   74

Parallel Object-Oriented Database Systems   78

6. PARALLEL KNOWLEDGE BASE SYSTEMS   83

Introduction   83

Parallel (Database) Production Systems   84

Parallel Deductive Database Systems   97

Parallel Active Database Systems   101

7. A PARALLEL OBJECT-ORIENTED KNOWLEDGE BASE SYSTEM   105

The Parallel Object-Oriented Data Model   105

The Abstract Machine   108

Parallel Query Processing   110

Parallel Rule Evaluation   118

8. CONCLUSIONS AND FUTURE DIRECTIONS   135

APPENDIX   139

References   141

Index   149

List of Figures/Tables

Figure 1. The rule spectrum and various rule integration schemata   14
Figure 2. The architecture of the DEVICE system   38
Figure 3. A sample complex event network   47
Figure 4. A negative event example   51
Figure 5. Hybrid memories of inter-object events   56
Figure 6. Sharing of conflict sets among the rule managers of DEVICE   59
Figure 7. Shared-everything architecture   71
Figure 8. Shared-nothing architecture   72
Figure 9. Hybrid architecture   73
Figure 10. Master-slave architecture   76
Figure 11. Parallel query execution   76
Figure 12. Non-uniform partitioning   77
Figure 13. A sample dependency graph   90
Figure 14. A cyclic read-write interference   90
Figure 15. A simple write-write interference   90
Figure 16. Instance hierarchy of PRACTIC objects   106
Figure 17. The hierarchical architecture of the abstract PRACTIC machine   108
Figure 18. A sample database schema   111
Figure 19. Horizontal partitioning of a class   113
Figure 20. Pipelined method execution   114
Figure 21. Hierarchical query execution   116
Figure 22. Hierarchical query execution with overlapping   117
Figure 23. Main loop of rule execution at each local rule manager   125
Figure 24. Auxiliary procedures for rule priority lock management   126
Figure 25. Auxiliary procedures for parallel rule processing   127
Table 1. ECA rule types handled by PRACTIC^{KB} 131

Foreword

It is a pleasure to me to commend this book. It brings together ideas about a number of different ways of organising computation that are often kept in separate compartments, namely Rule-based, Object-Oriented and Parallel computation. Each of them has seen great developments over the past two decades, but no one of them is a panacea, to be used to the exclusion of the others. This book compares their strengths and weaknesses and then makes a very clever synthesis of them to tackle the demanding problem of Knowledge-base management.

The history of database management systems (DBMS) has been a history of moving functionality from individual application programs in towards the shared kernel of the supporting system. First came indexing techniques for files, then query optimisation and then enforcement of integrity constraints. Constraints are themselves a form of high-level rule or knowledge, and this book argues that the maintenance and execution of other forms of rules (including Deductive rules, Production rules, Active rules) needs also to be done by a central shared facility, just as in a DBMS. Crucially, databases keep decisions on the physical details of data storage separate from the logical structure of data, and thus the KBMS kernel must also be free to change the physical details of rule storage and representation, so as to allow efficient, possibly parallel execution. This book explores ways to do this.

There is much to ponder on here, and we are still some years away from its widespread commercial application (although this book does discuss applications and is a step on the way towards it). As someone involved in database research for many years, I found this book a source of forward-thinking and stimulating ideas, and I am sure the reader will find this also!

Prof Peter M.D. Gray
University of Aberdeen, Scotland
October, 1997

Preface

Modern data intensive real-world applications, such as data warehousing, data mining, information retrieval, expert database systems, network management, etc. strive for advanced data representation, querying and programming facilities, in order to capture the increasing demand for efficient, automated, tolerant, intelligent and really useful information systems. Such information systems can only be supported by application developing tools that provide for complex representation and efficient processing of knowledge.

Knowledge Base Systems are an integration of conventional database systems with Artificial Intelligence techniques. Knowledge Base Systems provide inference capabilities to the database system by encapsulating the knowledge of the application domain within the database. Furthermore, Knowledge Base Systems provide sharing, ease of maintenance, and reusability of this knowledge which is usually expressed in the form of high-level, declarative rules, such as production and deductive rules.

However, the enormous amount and complexity of data and knowledge to be processed by these systems imposes the need for increased performance and expressiveness from the Knowledge Base System. The problems associated with the large volumes of data are mainly due to the sequential data processing and the inevitable input/output bottleneck. In order to avoid this bottleneck parallel database systems have emerged to speed-up data intensive applications.

Furthermore, the synchronous, sequential execution of large numbers of rules leads to unnecessarily many inferencing cycles that slow down Knowledge Base Systems. Parallel rule-based systems try to speed-up rule processing by executing asynchronously the various phases of rule evaluation in multiprocessor environments. Finally, the decision about the applicability of a certain piece of knowledge to a certain information state requires a large amount of pattern matching and control synchronization that can be distributed in a multiprocessor environment.

On the other hand, the structure complexity of the data and data manipulating programs, along with the impedance mismatch between the programming languages and the relational database management systems led to the advent of Object-Oriented Database systems, an intersection of object-oriented ideas and conventional databases. Object-Oriented Databases reduce the "semantic gap" between real world concepts and data representation models. This one-to-one mapping helps the development of complex applications, such as CAD/CAM, simulation, graphical user interfaces, etc. Object-Oriented Databases encapsulate within the database system both data and programs, with advantages such as program re-use, modularization, and ease of maintenance.

The object-oriented model offers a uniform, extensible and re-usable data and program representation that seems a promising solution for the integration of databases and knowledge-based systems. This book presents such an approach to Knowledge Base Systems: A Parallel Knowledge Base System that is built on top of a Parallel Active Object-Oriented Database System.

In the first part of the book, we discuss extensively the various attempts to integrate one or more rule types into databases in order to provide inferencing capabilities to the latter. The initial presentation of mostly sequential Knowledge Base Systems gives the reader a feel of the various problems and the proposed solutions for such systems. At the end of this first part, we present in detail one such system which integrates high-level, declarative rules into an active Object-Oriented Database. The resulting system is a flexible and extensible knowledge base system with multiple rule support.

In the second part of the book, we move into parallel Knowledge Base Systems by providing initial discussions of related research issues, such as parallel relational and object-oriented database systems. Many aspects of parallel rule execution are discussed including production, deductive, and active rules.

Finally, a complete parallel Knowledge Base System is presented. The system is based on the integration of a parallel Object-Oriented Database model with the multiple-rule integration scheme that is presented in the first part. The final system is implemented on a hierarchical multiprocessor architecture.

The book is intended as a reference text to the integration of database and knowledge base techniques for the researchers in the field of Knowledge Base Systems. It covers an extensive bibliography on the areas of rule integration in databases, namely active and deductive databases, as well as the unification of various rule types. Furthermore, the topics of parallel production, deductive, and active rule execution, both for databases and main-memory expert systems are reviewed.

Several chapters of the book (except probably of chapters 4 and 7 that describe a specific system) analyze in detail, using examples, various techniques for the above topics. Therefore, the book can also be used as a textbook for an advanced course in Knowledge Base Systems. Finally, the book gives an in-depth insight to a specific parallel Knowledge Base System for the researchers that work in the fields of Active Databases, Knowledge Bases, and Object-Oriented Databases, on the one hand, and Parallel Databases, on the other.

We would like to thank Professor Ahmed K. Elmagarmid who encouraged us to write this book and read an earlier draft of it. We are also grateful to Professor Peter M.D. Gray who kindly agreed to write the foreword for this book.

Part of this work was carried out while Dr. Vlahavas was on sabbatical leave at Purdue University. Dr. Bassiliades was supported during his PhD studies by a scholarship from the Greek Foundation of State Scholarships (F.S.S. - I.K.Y.).

1 INTRODUCTION

Knowledge, in terms of computer science, is the information about a specific domain needed by a computer program in order to exhibit a human-like (or in other words, intelligent) behavior over a specific problem. Knowledge includes both facts, i.e. data or static information about real-world entities and their properties, and relationships between them. Furthermore, knowledge can also be procedures on how to combine and operate on the above information.

Traditional computer programs exhibit a passive, pre-planned behavior that although efficiently performed is hardly flexible and adaptable to changing or unpredictable input patterns. Human-like behavior calls for easy adaptation to changing information about the environment and its processes. Computer programs that encapsulate such knowledge are called *knowledge-based systems*.

There are many important problems concerning the development of knowledge-based systems, such as where to find and how to collect the knowledge, how to represent the knowledge through a computer model, where to store and how to retrieve the knowledge, and, finally, how to process the knowledge in order to built efficient and fast applications.

Knowledge is usually collected from human experts through the knowledge acquisition process, performed by the knowledge engineer. The knowledge acquisition process is a very important and vast subject alone but is out of the scope of this book. The result of the knowledge acquisition phase is a semi-formal representation of the knowledge of the human expert in a certain application domain.

Knowledge is usually captured and programmed through non-deterministic, declarative programming languages, such as Prolog and OPS5. These languages allow the programmer to define in a highly descriptive manner the knowledge of a human expert about problems and their solutions. Furthermore, programs written in such languages can be extended easily because the data and program structures are more flexible and dynamic than the usual. Of course, the price to be paid for such flexibility is the decreased efficiency compared to more traditional approaches.

In order to increase the efficiency of knowledge-based systems various optimization techniques have been developed. These include efficient algorithms to retrieve, process and apply knowledge, along with using parallel algorithms to execute faster the new programs on multiprocessor machines. It turned out that the highly declarative nature of programming languages for knowledge-based systems is ideal for relaxing the user-programmer from the burden of deciding what optimizations and/or execution plans are needed to run his/her programs fast. It is the task of the system (i.e. the programmer of the programming tool) to decide how to execute the described program based on the availability of resources and the nature of the program.

Contemporary real-world computer applications try to model the complex and vast amount of the modern society's knowledge that must be handled by knowledge-based systems. Traditional applications also suffer from the existence of large amounts of data which are equivalent to facts in the context of knowledge-based systems. Their solution was to couple the programs that process data with special systems devoted to the efficient and reliable storage, retrieval and handling of data. These system are widely known as Database Management Systems (DBMSs).

The same trend is followed for knowledge-based systems where the management of knowledge has moved from the application to the Knowledge Base Management Systems (KBMS). KBMSs are an integration of conventional DBMSs with Artificial Intelligence techniques. KBMSs provide inference capabilities to the DBMS by allowing the encapsulation of the knowledge of the application domain within the database system. Furthermore, KBMSs provide sharing, ease of maintenance, and reusability of knowledge which is usually expressed in the form of high-level declarative rules, such as production and deductive rules.

The Knowledge Base System (KBS) consists of the KBMS along with a specific set of rules (called the *rule base*) and data (called the database). The rule base and the database of a KBS are collectively called the Knowledge Base (KB). In analogy, a Database System (DBS) consists of the DBMS and a specific set of data, called the database.

The performance problems of knowledge-based systems are much more evident in KBSs which have the additional disk IO overhead. The trend for both DBSs and KBSs is to use multiprocessor systems with multiple disks in order to beat the IO bottleneck problem of retrieving data sequentially from a single source. Furthermore, the processing of data and their relationships is done in parallel among the processors in order to decrease the total response time of the system.

An important role in the efficient processing of knowledge plays the correct and convenient knowledge representation. A good representation of the entities and their relationships involved in a problem may help to find a solution easier and/or faster. That is why so many knowledge representation techniques and numerous data models have appeared till now. The most prominent data models are the relational and object-oriented models, while the most influential knowledge representation techniques are production and logic rules, for dynamic knowledge, and semantic networks, conceptual graphs, and frames, for static knowledge.

Object-Oriented Database (OODB) systems are an intersection of object-oriented ideas and conventional, relational database systems. OODBs reduce the "semantic gap" between real world concepts and data representation models. This one-to-one mapping helps the development of applications that involve complex data structures and relationships among them, such as CAD/CAM, simulation, graphical user interfaces, etc.

OODBs encapsulate, within the database, both data and programs that manipulate data. The advantages of such an approach are obvious: program sharing, re-use, modularization, and ease of maintenance. The encapsulation of programs and the highly-structured data model of OODBs seems to be ideal for building KBMSs, although there are many researchers that argue that OODBs are highly procedural and cannot be integrated with the declarative languages of knowledge-based systems [139].

Frames, and other knowledge representation formalisms, that are extensively used in expert systems have many things in common with OODBs [111]. Furthermore, meta-classes and active rules provide a flexible platform over which the advanced functionality required by knowledge-based systems can be implemented [112]. For example, declarative rules can be easily integrated as first-class objects in an OODB, as we present in this book.

A recent trend to bridge the gap between knowledge base and database systems is active database systems. Active database systems constantly monitor system and user activities. When an interesting event happens they respond by executing certain procedures either related to the database or the environment. In this way the system is not a passive collection of data but also encapsulates management and data processing knowledge.

This re-active behavior is achieved through active rules which are a more low-level, procedural counterpart of the declarative rules used in knowledge-based systems. Active rules can be considered as primitive forms of knowledge encapsulated within the database; therefore, an active database system can be considered as some kind of KBS.

All rule paradigms are useful for different tasks in the knowledge base system. Therefore, the integration of multiple rule types in the same system is important. This will provide a single, flexible, multi-purpose knowledge base management system where users/programmers are allowed to choose the most appropriate format to express the application knowledge.

The objective of this book is to discuss all the existing approaches to building a KBMS by integrating one or more rule types in a DBMS. The book is mainly focused on the unification of all the existing rule paradigms under a common object-oriented framework. Such a uniform treatment provides the ability to add new rule types in the system easily by providing small, incremental changes to the rule semantics.

The book also discusses the issues related to increasing the performance of knowledge base systems by executing rules and/or processing data in parallel, in multiprocessor environments. Wherever necessary the book overviews issues related to knowledge base systems, such as database systems, expert systems, etc.

Finally, the book presents in detail a certain knowledge base system that integrates multiple rules types in an active OODB system. In addition, the integration of this system with a parallel OODB model is discussed. The resulting system is a highly flexible and efficient active object-oriented knowledge base system.

In the rest of this chapter we present the outline of the rest of the book. Finally, we give a brief description of the database terminology used both for relational and OODBs. Although the book is mainly concerned with OODBs there are many cases where issues related to relational databases are also discussed.

The book is divided into two parts. The first part discusses rule integration techniques into database systems, while the second discusses issues related to parallel database and knowledge base systems. More specifically, in chapter 2 we overview deductive and active databases which are two different research paths that have been followed towards the integration of rules in database systems. Not every possible theoretical and/or implementation detail of these systems is extensively presented but the focus is mainly on the issues needed for understanding the rest of the chapters.

In chapter 3 we present various techniques for unifying multiple rule types into a single system in order to provide flexible, multi-purpose knowledge bases. We mainly focus on the unification of production and deductive rule semantics and the integration of event-driven rules in declarative rules and vice-versa.

Finally, in the last chapter of the first part of the book (chapter 4), we present in detail the DEVICE system which integrates production and deductive rules into an active OODB system. This chapter presents the rule language, the compilation scheme, the rule matching algorithms, and the rule semantics of the DEVICE system. Furthermore, various practical issues are discussed, such as system architecture, implementation, optimization, and extensibility.

In the second part of the book we discuss issues related to parallel database and knowledge base systems. Chapter 5 overviews some of the issues of parallel relational and object-oriented database systems in order to make clear how these issues affect the integration of parallel knowledge base techniques. Issues such as parallel query processing algorithms, system architectures, and data distribution techniques are discussed.

Chapter 6 discusses the various theoretical issues and implementation details of the various approaches to parallel knowledge base systems. The discussion includes parallel production systems which although not directly related to databases give an insight to the problems emerging when executing rules in parallel, such as rule interference, serializability, and execution control. Finally, this chapter discusses some approaches to parallel deductive and active databases.

The second part concludes with chapter 7 which presents a parallel object-oriented knowledge base system, named PRACTIC^{KB}. The PRACTIC^{KB} system is an integration of a parallel OODB system, named PRACTIC, with the DEVICE knowledge base system. First the PRACTIC system is presented, in terms of its model, architecture, and query processing techniques. Then we discuss how the DEVICE algorithms are mapped onto the PRACTIC model, in terms of event and rule distribution, parallel rule matching, and execution algorithms.

Finally, chapter 8 concludes the book with brief summaries of the two parts and a discussion of current and future directions for both parallel and non-parallel knowledge base and active database systems.

Basic Terminology

In this section we give a brief introduction to the database terminology that will be used throughout the book. Although the book is mainly concerned with OODBs we also give a brief terminology for relational databases since these concepts are used occasionally throughout the book.

Relational Databases

The relational data model captures the relationships between entities and their properties. Data are represented through *relational tables*, which consist of a name, a description of their structure, and a set of *tuples* that obey the structure. The structure of a relation consists of a set of *attributes* which are the columns of the table and actually describe the properties of an entity. Each attribute has a name and a *data type*, i.e. the kind of data this attribute can be filled in with. For example, the following relation describes the employees of a company with many departments. Each attribute has a unique, simple type, i.e. a string, an integer, a date, etc.

```
EMP( NAME(string[20]), SALARY(integer),
     MANAGER(string([20]), DEPARTMENT(string([10])))
```

The tuples are the rows of the relational table and they stand for different entities that can be described under the same structure. For example, each employee of the company is a tuple of the EMP relation:

```
EMP('Nick',150000,'John','Accounting')
EMP('John',350000,'Jack','Accounting')
EMP('George',450000,'Mike','Manufacturing')
...
```

Tuples on a relation can either be unique, i.e. no two tuples can have exactly the same values in their attributes, or duplicates can exist. When duplicates are not allowed the relational tables are sets. Tuples are usually indexed by *keys* which are a combination of attributes (possibly one or even all) that uniquely identify each tuple. For example, if in the above simple EMP relation no two employees can have the same name, then the attribute name can be used as a key to access the tuples. Indirect access through an index is usually faster than direct, sequential access of the table because indexes are organized in tree-like data structures.

Database systems that are based on the relational model need a data definition language to allow the description of relation structures (also called *database schema*) and a data manipulation language to allow the user to issue *ad-hoc queries* (data retrieval) and to modify (or update) data. The most popular such language is SQL. A query in SQL looks like the following:

```
SELECT name,salary
FROM emp
WHERE department='Accounting'
```

The above query searches throughout the relation in the FROM clause to find tuples that satisfy the criteria in the WHERE clause. This is called *selection*. The result of this query will not be the entire tuples that pass the selection criteria but only the two attributes found in the SELECT clause. This is called *projection*.

Selection and projection are two of the *relational operators*. Other relational operators are join, union, and difference. The two latter are the usual operations on sets. *Join* is an operation that combines the tuples of two (or more) relations into a new relation, based on one (or more) common attributes between the two relations. For example, consider the DEPT relation that describes information about the company departments in our simple company database:

```
DEPT(NAME(string[10]),ADDRESS(string([25])))
```

The following SQL query joins the two relations based on the existence of the departments name in attributes of both relations:

```
SELECT e.name,d.address
FROM emp e, dept d
WHERE e.salary>250000 AND e.department=d.name
```

More on relational databases can be found in various popular textbooks, such as [45, 107, 138]. Some more details will be given in the following chapters, whenever needed.

Object-Oriented Databases

OODBs can be considered as an extension of relational databases with concepts from object-oriented programming. *Objects* are independent entities that encapsulate both their internal state and their behavior. The internal state of objects is the actual data and can be paralleled with tuples. The behavior of objects is a set of procedures or programs that act upon the data and are called *methods*. Methods have a *signature* which is their name and the type of input and output arguments. The set of methods defines the interface through which all interactions with a certain objects takes place.

Object *encapsulation* and independence leads to message passing as the major computation model. Programs and queries for OODBs are uniformly encoded through a sequence of messages. *Messages* are actually procedure calls which are evaluated by the *message recipient* objects. The object that sends the message does not know and does not care about the implementation of the procedure call (i.e. the message) but only for the functionality and results that this provides.

There are three types of objects, in OODBs: a) instance objects, which are the actual data, b) classes, which are abstract descriptions of the structure and behavior of instances, and c) meta-classes, which are abstract descriptions of classes.

Objects are linked to each other through relationships. The most basic is the
is_instance_of relationship that links instance objects with their classes and
classes with their meta-classes. For example, consider the following example:

```
class              person
is_instance_of     class
attributes         name(string[20])
                   birthdate(integer)
                   friends(list_of person)
methods            get_age ::= (today()-self.birthdate)/365

instance           10#person
is_instance_of     person
name               'Nick'
birthdate          09051969
friends            [11#person,22#person,33#person]
```

The class person is an instance of the meta-class class which is a generic
meta-class of the system. The object 10#person is an instance of class person.
The objects are uniquely identified through an object identifier (OID). For classes
and meta-classes the OID is their name, while for instance objects the OID is
generated by the system.

The OID is used for sending messages to an object or to link objects through user-
defined relationships. For example, the following is a message[1] sent to object
10#person to retrieve the age:

```
get_age(Age)  ⇒  10#person
```

The attribute friends of class person is a multi-valued attribute, i.e. an
attribute whose value is not a simple data element but a list of elements. This is a
very important difference of OODBs with relational databases. Furthermore, each of
the elements of this list is not a simple data type, such as an integer, but the OID of
other person objects. In this way user-defined relationships between objects are
defined.

Complex objects are objects that are related to other objects using the user-defined
relationships. The attributes that implement these relationships are called *complex
attributes* and they are filled with OIDs or pointers to other objects. The complex
object is the collection of all these interrelated objects and is usually represented by
the top-level objects which is the one that begins the chain of the relationship.

---

[1] We will use the message sending notation of an OODB named ADAM [109]
throughout the book.

Finally, there exists the is_a relationship which specializes the structure and behavior of a class (called super-class) into another class (called sub-class). A sub-class inherits all attribute and method definitions of its super-class, unless otherwise specified. The is_a relationship defines a class inheritance hierarchy. The set of all the instances of a class is called its extension. The *class extension* is a subset of the extensions all its super-classes. For example, consider the following class emp which is a subclass of class person and inherits all the attributes and methods defined above:

```
class            emp
is_instance_of   class
is_a             person
attributes       manager(emp)
                 salary(integer)
methods          get_tax ::= self.salary * 15%
```

An instance of class emp can receive messages both for its own defined methods and the methods defined for its super-classes. Furthermore, a method defined at a super-class can be overridden by a more specific method or even partially inherited.

More details on OODBs will be given in chapter 7. Furthermore, there exist numerous books on OODBs, such as [71, 95], that present the topic in detail, including research issues concerning query languages and efficiency, and review several commercial and research prototype OODB systems.

PART I KNOWLEDGE BASE SYSTEMS
Rule Integration in Databases

In this part of the book, we describe various techniques for integrating rules into database systems which results into Knowledge Base Systems. We mainly focus on the unification of multiple rule types into a single system in order to provide flexible, multi-purpose knowledge bases. Finally, we present in detail DEVICE, an active object-oriented knowledge base system that integrates multiple declarative rule types into an active object-oriented database that generically supports only procedural event-driven rules.

2 DEDUCTIVE AND ACTIVE DATABASES

In this chapter we overview deductive and active databases which are the two different paths that have been followed towards the integration of rules in database systems. We do not extensively present every theoretical and/or implementation detail of these systems, but we mainly focus on the issues that will prove useful for the understanding of the unification of various rule systems that will be discussed in the next chapter.

Introduction: The Rule Spectrum

Knowledge Base Management Systems (KBMSs) are normal Database Management Systems (DBMSs) extended with some kind of knowledge. *Knowledge* usually means some kind of declarative language, and takes the form of rules [138]. According to which rule type has been integrated into a DBMS, we distinguish between two types of KBMS: deductive and active database systems.

Deductive databases [33, 102, 138] use declarative logic programming style rules (also called *deductive rules*) that add the power of recursively defined views to conventional databases. Deductive rules declaratively describe new, derived data in terms of existing data, without an exact description of how new data are created or treated.

On the other hand, active database systems extend traditional database systems with the ability to perform certain operations automatically in response to certain situations that occur in the database. For this reason they use low-level *situation-*

action rules (also called *active rules*) which are triggered when a *situation* arises in the database. As a consequent a set of *actions* is performed on the database. Active rules are used to provide various functionalities to the database system, such as database integrity constraints, views and derived data, authorization, statistics gathering, monitoring and alerting, knowledge bases and expert systems, workflow management, etc. Active rules can take the form of *data-driven* or *event-driven* rules.

Data-driven or *production* rules are more declarative than event-driven rules [78] because their *situation* part is a declarative description of a firing situation (a query) without an exact definition of how or when this situation is detected.

Event-driven or Event-Condition-Action (*ECA*) rules are more procedural because they explicitly define their triggering situation [144]. Specifically, ECA rules are triggered by an *event* that occurs inside or outside the system, then a *condition* is checked to verify the triggering context and, finally, the *actions* are executed.

Despite the differences of the above rule types in their syntax, semantics, use, and implementation, it has been proposed by Widom [144] that active and deductive rules are not distinct but rather form a spectrum of various rule paradigms. Widom has described a general common framework under which all rule types found in the literature can be placed by adapting slightly the framework. Figure 1 shows how the above rule types fit into the rule spectrum.

All rule paradigms are useful in an active KBMS. Therefore, the unification of the various rule types in a single system is an important research task that has received considerable attention over the recent literature (Figure 1).

According to Widom, rule types that lie closer to the higher-level edge of the rule spectrum can be translated into (and, therefore, emulated by) lower-level rule types. Furthermore, the semantics of high-level rules can be extended to cover the

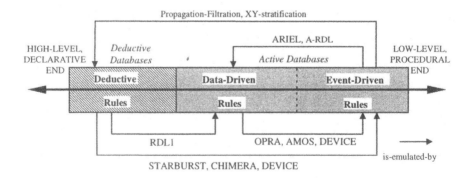

Figure 1. The rule spectrum and various rule integration schemata

semantics of lower-level rules, so that the latter can be used in a system that supports a high-level rule system.

In the following sections of this chapter, we present in more detail various approaches to deductive and active databases, and, in the following chapter, we discuss various techniques to unify some or all of the above rule types.

Deductive Databases

A deductive database [33, 138] incorporates aspects of logic programming and thereby provides advantages over pure relational systems (RDBs) by bridging the gap towards knowledge bases. Deductive databases allow users, through the means of deductive rules, to deduce facts concerning data stored in the database.

A deductive database consists of an extensional database (EDB) and an intentional database (IDB). The former (also called *base data*) is actually a relational database which is equivalent to the set of all facts in a Prolog program. The latter is the set of all facts that are derived through the application of deductive rules on the EDB.

There are two approaches to implementing deductive databases:

- coupling an RDB with a logic programming system, usually Prolog, or

- extending a relational query language with deductive language features, usually Datalog and its extensions.

The latter solution achieves a greater integration and much less interaction overhead between the logic programming and the database system, while it allows the rule programmer to use all of the advantages of conventional database systems. In addition, the integration of logic programming features into the relational framework was not a difficult task, since logic underlies the relational data model (relational calculus).

Datalog is a logic programming language designed for use as a database language. It is non-procedural, set-oriented, with no order sensitivity, no special predicates, and no function symbols. Datalog eliminates the most important drawbacks of Prolog, keeping its simple syntax.

Datalog programs are built from deductive rules. A rule is built from *atomic formulas*, which are predicate symbols (relation names) with a list of arguments (relation attributes). A Datalog rule consists of the *head* (also called conclusion or consequent) and the *body* (also called condition or antecedent). The head consists of a single atomic formula, while the body can contain more than one positive or negative atomic formulas connected through logical conjunction:

$$a(X,Y) \ :- \ b(X,Z), \ c(Z,Y).$$

The database interpretation of a Datalog rule is that *if the condition of the rule is satisfied, then the tuple(s) described by the head of the rule should be in the database*. The head predicate a is called IDB predicate, while b, c can either be EDB predicates (base relations) or IDB predicates. For example, if c is an IDB predicate in the above rule, then it might be defined using a rule like the following:

$$c(X,Y) \ :- \ e(X,Y,a), \ d(Y).$$

When a predicate appears in the body of another predicate, then we say that the latter *depends* on the former. The *dependency graph* of a Datalog program is a graph whose nodes are all the IDB predicates of a set of rules and two nodes are connected through a directed arc if one depends upon the other.

When a predicate appears both in the head and the body of a rule, then this rule is called *recursive rule*. Recursive programs can exist even when no recursive rules exist. This happens when two predicates depend on each other, either directly or indirectly through a chain or rules. A *cycle* in the dependency graph indicates a recursive program.

The evaluation of Datalog programs consists of finding the minimal set of facts that are derivable from IDB rules and EDB facts. The most popular evaluation technique is *semi-naive evaluation*. Semi-naive evaluation is a *bottom-up* evaluation technique, i.e. the evaluation proceeds from the known EDB facts towards all the derivable IDB facts, much alike forward chaining in production systems (see the next section about *Data-driven Rules*).

Initially, the EDB facts that appear in the bodies of deductive rules are combined to produce the first set of IDB facts. Then these IDB facts that appear in the bodies of other rules along with the existing EDB facts are used to produce new IDB facts and so on and so forth until no more IDB facts are produced. During any cycle of the computation only the newly derived IDB facts are considered.

When negation is allowed in the body of Datalog rules then theoretical problems are introduced, unless a syntactic restriction, called *stratification*, is enforced. A program is stratified when there are no cycles in the dependency graph that include negated atomic formulas. To be more specific, consider the following rule:

$$p(X,Y) \ :- \ t(X,Y), \ \neg q(Y).$$

where ¬ denotes negation of the successive atomic formula. This rule is stratified if there is not a path from p to q in the dependency graph.

Safe rules are the ones that have the following properties: a) variables that appear in the head must also appear at least once inside a non-negated condition and b) variables that are used inside a negated condition must also appear at least once inside a non-negated condition. Non-safe rules create the problem of *infinite* IDB relations.

If a program is stratified then a *stratum* is assigned to each of its IDB predicates. The stratum is a positive integer number that imposes an order of evaluation for the IDB predicates. In a rule where negation appears in the body, the stratum of the head predicate must be strictly greater than the stratum of the negated predicate, while in a rule with only positive atomic formulas the stratum of all predicates can be at most equal. The evaluation of safe, stratified programs proceeds from EDB facts and IDB predicates with stratum 1, then IDB predicates with stratum 2 and so on so forth until a fixpoint is reached.

Semi-naive evaluation is appropriate when the user is interested in all derivable facts. However, some times the user may want, through a selection query, a subset of the above complete set. In these cases, especially when the EDB is a huge database, it is not very efficient to compute all the derivable facts and then select only those that match the user's query. Various re-writing techniques, such as *magic sets*, have been proposed to optimize the evaluation process with respect to a certain query [33].

The magic sets method considers the *adornment* of a certain query, i.e. the set of bound and free variables of the query. Using this information, and the definition of the rule, one can "pass" the bound variables from the head of the rule to the subgoals of the body. These subgoals, in turn, can "pass" the potential bindings to their definition rules and so on and so forth until the EDB predicates are reached. This is called *sideways information passing* and it is the normal procedure followed by top-down evaluation techniques, such as Prolog.

In order to emulate the binding passing strategy of top-down methods, the magic sets method introduces some extra predicates (along with their definition rules) as subgoals in the body of the existing deductive rules. These *magic predicates*, during the bottom-up evaluation, constrain the values that the variables can take according to the initial query adornment that has been propagated to all branches of the derivation tree; therefore, the new set of rules is more efficient with respect to the specific query.

We will not expand any further on deductive databases here since they are a very well studied research area. The purpose of this section was not to present deductive databases extensively but to introduce informally some of their conceptr that will help the reader to follow the unification of other rule types with deductive rules.

The most successful and influential deductive database systems are ADITI [140], CORAL [116], GLUE-NAIL [48], and LDL [40]. More details about theoretical issues of deductive databases and descriptions of the above or other systems can be found in [33] and [138].

Deductive Object-Oriented Databases

New applications of database technology, such as design and concurrent engineering applications, integration of heterogeneous, independent databases, applications involving multimedia data, etc., require advanced data representation features, such as object-orientation. The integration of deductive databases with OODBs, called Deductive Object-Oriented Databases (DOOD), reflects the growing need of both designers and users for a representation tool that is semantically richer than that provided by RDBs, as well as to the widely acknowledged benefits of using logic as a tool for the formalization of both the static and the dynamic aspects of databases.

Though these two formalisms have been regarded as in opposition [139], indeed they can be integrated within a single approach which selects compatible features and merges them into a unique setting [58]. The feasibility of such an approach has been shown both at a theoretical [3, 93] and at an implementation level [30].

There are several approaches to the integration of deductive and object-oriented databases [58]. They mostly fall into three categories: a) object-oriented (OO) extensions to Datalog, such as [2, 3], b) OO extensions to Prolog, such as [101, 109, 151], and c) OO extensions to first-order logic programming [39, 92, 93].

The most notable disadvantage of approaches in categories a) and c) is that they represent theoretical departures from logic, therefore their usability and practicality in terms of object-oriented features is limited. On the other hand, approaches of extending Prolog with OO features usually bring full-featured OO systems with the additional benefit of the existence of an underlying high-level language. However, Prolog is mostly used as a medium for meta-programming OO features and is not smoothly integrated with the OO model.

Some more recent approaches to unifying deductive and object-oriented databases, such as [18, 72], follows an opposite direction by extending an OODB with deductive capabilities. This brings full OO functionality into the system and has the additional merits of using deductive rules for deriving new objects from the stored ones. The integration has been achieved by emulating deductive rules using one or more ECA rules. More details will be described in chapters 3 and 4.

Ullman's objections to DOODs. Ullman [139] has a raised a number of issues against the unification of deductive and object-oriented databases in a single DOOD system.

Derived objects by different proofs. Assume that the following recursive definition of path from the arcs of a graph defines a set of derived objects:

```
path(X,Y)  :- arc(X,Y).
path(X,Y)  :- path(X,Z), arc(Z,Y).
```

Ullman argued that if there are multiple derivations for a single path(X,Y) tuple then a different object for each such path should be created. This gives a different semantics from deductive relational databases where a value based interpretation would inhibit the creation of multiple tuples when a single path has multiple derivations.

However, Ullman's argument uses path with two different meanings. In deductive relational databases, path is an entity that describes the existence of a connection between two nodes, whereas in DOOD it denotes the connection between two nodes *through a sequence of intermediate points* [58].

Types of derived objects. Assume the following rule, where b, c are EDB relations (or classes), while a is an IDB relation (or class).

```
a(X,Y,Z)  :- b(X,Z), c(Z,Y).
```

The type of b and c relations (classes) is well-defined from the database schema, whereas the type of the derived relation (class) a should be dynamically defined when the above rule is created.

In deductive relational databases all the relational operations are immediately available for the new type, whereas in DOODs it is not clear which operations will be available, in addition to the generic operations on objects.

This dynamic typing problem has been addressed by researchers on object-oriented view definitions resulting in some very successful and elegant solutions [1, 19, 125] that place a dynamically defined class (view) in an existing class hierarchy. This allows the derived class to inherit the behavior of pre-existing classes.

Query optimization. Declarative languages, such as SQL and Datalog, are easily optimizable because the semantics of all operations are predetermined. OODBs, however, can have arbitrarily defined operations (methods) whose semantics are veiled by encapsulation.

Two solutions to the above problem have been proposed. The first was proposed by Ullman himself and suggests the optimization of queries involving only generic operations with known semantics, such as selection, projection, and join. Another solution is to optimize methods, too, by asking the database to reveal certain information about methods that would help an optimizer to include methods in the optimization process [89].

Active Databases

An *Active Database System* (ADB) is a conventional, passive database system extended with the capability of reactive behavior. This means that the system can perform certain operations automatically, in response to certain situations that have occurred in the database.

An ADB is significantly more powerful than its passive counterpart because it can achieve the following:

- perform functions that in passive databases systems must be encoded in applications;

- facilitate applications beyond the scope of passive database systems;

- perform tasks that require special-purpose subsystems in passive database systems.

The desired active behavior of ADBs is usually specified using *active rules*. There is a certain confusion about the term "active rules"; some researchers [78, 79] denote by this term the production rules met in expert system technology [59, 60], while others refer to the Event-Condition-Action (ECA) rules [36, 46, 57, 64] met in many active database systems.

Henceforth, we will use the term *active rules* to denote both these rule types collectively. Furthermore, we will use the above specific terms to address to each of the two active rule types in order to avoid the confusion:

- Production or "data-driven" rules are the rules of the form:

```
IF condition THEN action
```

The condition of these rules describe data states that should be reached by the database. When the condition is satisfied the production rule is fired (or triggered) and its set of actions is executed against the database.

- ECA or "event-driven" rules have the following form:

```
ON event IF condition THEN action
```

The ECA rule is explicitly triggered when the event of the rule has been detected, either in the database, caused by a data manipulation operator or externally by another system. The condition of the rule is only then checked and if satisfied the rule action is executed.

Typically, ADB systems support only one of the above two active rule types. However, there are few systems that support both ones. In the following sections we will present some implementation issues for the systems that support only one active rule type. In the next chapter we will discuss some techniques for integrating these two rule types.

Event-Driven Rules

There are several ADB systems in the literature that support event-driven or ECA rules. Among these systems are the most of the active OODBs, such as HIPAC [46], SENTINEL [36], REACH [26], ADAM/EXACT [56, 57], SAMOS [64], AMOS [121], ACOOD [22], and NAOS [41]. The main reason for this is that ECA rules are the most "natural" choice for generic rule support since events conform to the message-passing paradigm of object-oriented computation and every recognizable message/method can be a potential event. Therefore, ECA rule execution can be very easily implemented as a "detour" from normal method execution.

For example, assume that there is a class emp that describes employees of a corporation and an employee that is an instance of this class with object identifier (OID) 14#emp. If someone wants to insert a value to the attribute salary of this employee then the following message should be sent to the instance object:

$$put\_salary([300000]) \Rightarrow 14\#emp$$

where put_salary is the name of a corresponding method defined at class emp that inserts the method parameter in the salary attribute of class instances.

Just before and/or right after the put_salary method is executed there is an opportunity to check if there is an event that should be monitored for this method and class. If there is, then the event occurrence is detected and signaled to the event manager of the system. Method execution proceeds normally between the two event detection phases. Therefore, event detection can be easily implemented as a side-effect of the normal OODB method execution mechanism.

In addition to database operations, events can be also happenings of interest external to the database, e.g. clock events or operating system events (interrupts). Furthermore, events can be both *simple* or *primitive*, as the ones we have presented, and *complex* or *compound*. Complex events are combinations of simple events through event constructors, such as conjunction, disjunction, sequence, periodical, etc. Complex events are useful for integrating temporal aspects in an active database or for expressing complex logical conditions, as in SNOOP/SENTINEL [37], SAMOS [63], and ODE [67]. Furthermore, in chapter 4 we will show how complex events have been used in DEVICE to integrate declarative rules into an active database [16].

All of the above OODB systems, more or less, follow this event detection and active rule execution scheme. A notable exception is ODE [66] where *triggers* (the equivalent to ECA rules) must be explicitly evoked by member functions and are not automatically detected by the system.

On the other hand, in relational databases, there are a number of different implementation techniques. This is mainly due to the fact that relational databases have a number of predefined generic operations that are common to all relations. Therefore, it would be quite inefficient to check for events every time a generic operation, such as insert or delete, is executed on any relation.

One of the first relational database systems to support ECA rules are POSTGRES [115] and STARBURST [145]. POSTGRES uses a tuple marking technique where each tuple that is a candidate to trigger an ECA rule is permanently marked by a *rule lock* that indicates which rule will be triggered at run-time. Some times a rule lock is placed on the relation instead, when the granularity of the rule cannot be determined at rule-creation time or for space-saving purposes. At run-time, the tuple that is "modified" is checked for rule locks, and the appropriate rules are then executed.

STARBURST uses its extended features (such as *attachment procedures* which is a concept similar to *demons* in the technology of frame-based expert system) in order to log the operations that trigger ECA rules. At the end of the transaction or at user-specified *checkpoints* the rule manager collects the triggered rules from the log and executes them.

Finally, A-RDL [128] and ARIEL [78] support events and ECA rules on top of production rules using delta-relations, a technique that will be described thoroughly in the next chapter.

Coupling modes. An important aspect of ECA rule execution is the exact time of event detection, condition checking, and action execution relative to the triggering operation and the end of the transaction. For example, there can be various delays in checking the condition of a rule after its event is detected. Or the execution of a rule's action can be delayed after its condition is verified. These possibilities are called rule *coupling modes.*

There are three coupling modes, both for the relative delay between event detection and condition checking (EC coupling) and between condition checking and action execution (CA coupling):

- *Immediate.* There is no delay between the evaluation/execution of the next ECA rule part. For example, the action is executed immediately after the condition is satisfied.

- *Deferred.* The evaluation/execution of the next ECA rule part is delayed until the end of the current transaction. For example, the condition of the rule is not checked after its event has been signaled but at the end of the transaction. This coupling mode may prove useful for e.g. checking integrity constraints, where many single updates violate the constraint but the overall effect is a valid transaction. If the condition is checked immediately after the first "illegal" update then a constraint violation will be detected, while if the check is delayed until the end of the transaction, the constraint violation might be repaired by following updates.

- *Decoupled.* The evaluation/execution of the next ECA rule part is done in a separate transaction that might or might not depend on the current transaction. This mode is useful when long chains of rules are triggered and it is preferable to decompose it into smaller transactions to increase the database concurrency and availability.

A more detailed description of the concepts and features of ADBs can be found in the *Active Database Manifesto* [42]. Most of the above ADB systems can be found in an excellent collection of ADB research prototypes [146]. Here we have tried to introduce some of the concepts of active rules and present some implementation details about various active rule systems that will help our later discussion of multiple rule integration.

Data-Driven Rules

Several active relational database systems, such as RPL [47], RDL1 [91], DIPS [126], DATEX [27], and ARIEL [78] support production rules, in the fashion of OPS5-like expert systems.

All the above systems base their operation on the MATCH-SELECT-ACT cycle of production rule systems [59]. More specifically, production systems consist of a) the *working memory* (WM) that holds the initial data of a problem, plus the intermediate and final results, and b) the *production memory* that holds the production rules. In analogy, the working memory of database production systems is the database itself while the production rules are kept in the system's rule dictionaries.

During the MATCH phase of the *production cycle* the system checks which rule conditions match with data in the working memory. A rule whose condition has been successfully matched against the working memory and its variables have been replaced by actual values is called *rule instantiation.* Production systems execute only one rule instantation per cycle; therefore, when more than one rule instantations are matched, they are all placed in the *conflict set* in order to be considered later for selection.

During the SELECT phase the system selects a single rule instantation from the conflict set based on various *conflict resolution criteria.* Finally, the selected rule instantation is executed in the ACT phase. The actions of the production rule may cause additional rule instantations to be inserted or removed from the conflict set. The same procedure is continued until there are no more rule instantations left in the conflict set after a MATCH phase.

One of the most important bottlenecks in the performance of production systems is the MATCH phase. The naive approach is to match all production rule conditions against all working memory elements at each cycle. However, various algorithms have been proposed that incrementally decide which rules should be added to or removed from the conflict set, such as RETE [60], TREAT [103], A-TREAT [78], GATOR [77], and LEAPS [27].

Almost all of the above algorithms are based on the compilation of the production rule conditions into a graph that is called *discrimination network* which accepts in its input the modifications that occurred in the working memory and output the rule instantations that should be added to or removed from the conflict set. The discrimination network usually maintains some information on the previously inserted elements in order to decide if the new elements combined with the previous ones make some rules match.

The RETE network maintains one α-memory for each test in the condition in order to store all database tuples that pass this test. This filtering reduces the amount of tuples to be joined due to shared variables in the condition. The following is a sample production rule whose condition refers to relations a, b. There are 2 selections conditions, one for each relation, and one join on the X variable.

```
IF a(1,X) and b(X,2) THEN <action>
```

The RETE network also maintains one β-memory for each join in the condition to store all combined tuples that pass the join. The information for each propagated tuple inside the RETE network is called *token*. The last β-memory outputs a token that covers the whole condition and indicates that a rule has been selected.

A more detailed description of a RETE-like discrimination network will be presented in chapter 4.

The rest of the discrimination networks are variations of RETE. For example, the TREAT network does not have β-memories but multi-way joins are performed directly between the α-memory tokens and the database relations.

Most of the database production rule systems, that we mentioned at the beginning of this section, use some kind of discrimination network. More specifically, RPL uses a main-memory variation of RETE; RDL1 uses a special petri net called *Production Compilation Network* [100]; DIPS uses a novel, efficient rule condition matching algorithm that stores a "compressed" variation of the RETE network tokens into relational tables; finally, ARIEL uses the A-TREAT algorithm which uses virtual α-memories to save some space compared to TREAT, along with special selection predicate indices for speeding-up the testing of selection conditions of rules.

In contrast, DATEX uses a complicated marking scheme [27], like POSTGRES, which employs a number of different indices to guide the search for matching first selection conditions and then to perform joins to the appropriate direction of the condition. However, we believe that the same general principles apply to both the LEAPS algorithm and the discrimination network algorithms, and the only conceptual difference, in LEAPS, is that the discrimination network is not centralized but distributed across several persistent data structures. Of course, this distribution has certain benefits concerning the space and time complexity of the algorithm compared to the discrimination network algorithms.

Finally, we remind that the A-RDL [128] extension of RDL1 and ARIEL support the matching of transitional conditions using delta-relations. Thus, they provide a means to emulate events and ECA rules on top of production rules. A thorough discussion of this technique can be found in the next chapter.

3 INTEGRATION OF MULTIPLE RULE TYPES

In the previous chapter we have presented the integration of various rule types in various database systems. All rule paradigms are useful for different tasks in the database system. Therefore, the integration of multiple rule types in the same system is important. This will provide a single, flexible, multi-purpose knowledge base management system.

In this chapter we present various techniques for unifying two or more different rule paradigms. More specifically, recall Figure 1 from the previous chapter where the systems that attempt to integrate multiple rule types using a common framework are shown along with arcs that indicate which rules are the generic ones and which are emulated using the former. In this chapter we classify the integration attempts into three major categories: a) unification of production and deductive rule semantics, b) integration of ECA rules in declarative rule systems, and c) integration of declarative rules into active database systems that support ECA rules only.

Unification of Production and Deductive Rule Semantics

The RDL1 system [91, 100] discussed in the previous chapter made an important contribution to the unification of production and deductive rule semantics. More specifically, the production rule language of RDL1 has been proved to be as expressive as Datalog with negation [100].

The condition of an RDL1 production rule is a range restricted formula of the relational calculus, as in Datalog, while the action can be a set of positive or negative literals. A positive literal means the insertion of the corresponding tuple in the database while the negative literal means deletion. In contrast, Datalog allows only a single positive literal in the head which is equivalent to the RDL1 rule action.

According to the semantics of deductive rules, as described by Widom in [144], when the condition of the deductive rule is satisfied, then the tuple/object described by the rule head "is in the relation" of the head's predicate. There can be two interpretations, according to the materialized and the non-materialized approaches to deductive databases.

If the derived relation/class (IDB) is materialized then the derived tuple/object must be inserted in the database (procedural action). Otherwise, according to the non-materialized approach, the derived tuple/object is inserted in the answer set of the query that evoked the rule processing algorithm. We can safely consider that the answer set is a temporarily materialized derived relation which is deleted after the answer to the query. Therefore, for both approaches, the operational semantics of the bottom-up processing of deductive rules can be compared to forward chaining production rules.

Thus, production and deductive rules differ only in their consequent/action part while the condition part is a declarative query over the database for both. The action part of a production rule is an explicit set of procedural database modifications while the consequent part of a deductive rule is an implicit action of object creation. Henceforth, we will not distinguish between them and we will collectively call them *declarative rules*.

Integration of ECA Rules in Declarative Rule Conditions

ECA rules are low-level rules that describe explicitly their activation time. For example, the following rule does not allow any employees named 'Mike' which earn more than 500000 to be inserted to the relation emp:

```
ON    APPEND emp
IF    emp.name='Mike' and emp.sal>500000
THEN  DELETE emp
```

Production and deductive rules, on the other hand, do not explicitly describe when they are activated. Instead, their declarative condition states that if somehow, at some point, the situation is met in the database, the rule is activated. Therefore, a generic difference between the event description of ECA rules and the condition of declarative rules is that the former describes a *change* in the state of the database while the latter describes a static database state.

In order to integrate events in the condition of declarative rules a new construct is needed to describe dynamic changes in the database instead of static conditions. This construct is *delta relations*. A delta relation consists of the tuples of a relation that have been changed during the current transaction or between rule checkpoints.

There are various delta relations for each normal database relation to reflect the various changes that can be applied to any given relation. For example, for a relation $R(A_1, \ldots, A_n)$ there exist three delta relations [127]:

1. `inserted_R(A₁,...,Aₙ)`, for the tuples that have been inserted to relation R,

2. `deleted_R(A₁,...,Aₙ)`, for the deleted tuples, and

3. `updated_R(ᵒˡᵈA₁,...,ᵒˡᵈAₙ,ⁿᵉʷA₁,...,ⁿᵉʷAₙ)`, for the tuples that have been updated, where keywords `old, new`, denote the old and the new values of the corresponding attribute, respectively.

Delta relations are transient relations that hold data modifications during a transaction. After the transaction is committed these relations are flashed into their normal counterparts.

Using delta relations the ECA rule that has been presented at the beginning of this section can be expressed as the following production rule:

```
IF    e IN inserted_emp and e.name='Mike' and
      e.sal>500000
THEN  DELETE e
```

The above rule can be used interchangeably with the ECA rule at the section beginning.

The technique of delta relations has been used by most systems that integrate events in either production or deductive rules. For example, ARIEL [78] and A-RDL [127] are mainly production database rule systems that also support the use of ECA rules using delta relations. Of course, their approaches are slightly different from the one that has been described here.

ARIEL allows the definition of both production and ECA rules. However the conditions of either rule types cannot refer to the delta relations directly. Instead, delta relations are used by the low-level mechanism to "translate" the event into a condition reference to a delta relation. Of course, transition conditions can be expressed, i.e. the condition can explicitly refer to old and new values of a tuple.

A-RDL, on the other hand, does not allow the ECA rule syntax, i.e. events cannot be defined explicitly. It allows only the production rule syntax with explicit reference to delta relations, which is equivalent to event definition. Exactly the same concept is used in the integration of active and deductive rules using the Propagation-Filtration algorithm [80].

Another approach to unifying active and deductive rules is through XY-stratification [152]. XY-stratification keeps track of the stratum each derivation was in while it copies all the derivations from a previous stratum to a new. In this way it is easy to deduce at each stratum which are the new derivations. This is very similar to the delta relations we presented above.

Updates and events can be easily added to the language through the definition of an event queue. Each update request is appended to the event queue predicate and each IDB predicate at each stratum considers the events (updates) that have been queued at the previous stratum, in addition to the updates that occur due to the logical, XY-stratified rules. In this way external updates, as well as production and ECA rules can be very easily incorporated into the deductive rule language.

Despite the serious theoretical groundness of XY-stratification, we believe that is conceptually no different than delta relations since it is also based on the incremental detection of changes to relations through consecutive database states (or fixpoints).

Integration of Declarative Rules in Active Databases

ECA rules are the most low-level rule type of the rule spectrum (Figure 1); therefore, they provide the most programming constructs for implementing add-on features with various functionality in active databases. Production and deductive rules, on the other hand, are high-level programming tools with simple, declarative semantics which is only a subset of the semantics that can be expressed with ECA rules. Of course, declarative rules in return are easier for a naive user to use than ECA rules.

The limited functionality of declarative rules can be easily "emulated" by ECA rules. The reason to do so is that a single system could provide all kinds of rule programming paradigms for different user categories.

There are two approaches to integrating declarative rules into ECA rules: the *multi-rule* and the *single-rule* approaches. Both are based on the compilation of a declarative rule into one or more ECA rules. The ECA rules are then triggered by data modification events and they act accordingly in order to implement the semantics of declarative rules. In the rest of this section we present and compare these two declarative rule compilation techniques.

The Multi-Rule Approach

According to the multi-rule scheme, each declarative rule is translated into many ECA rules. Each ECA rule is triggered by a different, simple event which is derived from a single condition element of the condition of the declarative rule. The condition of each ECA rule is almost the same as the condition of the declarative rule, minus the event.

This technique has been proposed both for production rules [110, 129] and deductive rules [35, 72].

Production rules. Consider the following production rule:

$$P_1: \text{IF a \& b \& c THEN } <action>$$

where a, b, c are testing patterns for data items (tuples, objects, etc.) which we will be called, henceforth, just *data items* for brevity. Notice that these patterns can include variables, even shared among the patterns, which are not shown in this and the next rule examples. The above rule is compiled into the following 3 ECA rules:

```
EP₁: ON insert(a)  IF b & c THEN <action>
EP₂: ON insert(b)  IF a & c THEN <action>
EP₃: ON insert(c)  IF a & b THEN <action>
```

The event insert(x) is a primitive event which is detected and signaled when the data item x is inserted in the database.

These three ECA rules suffice to monitor the database for the satisfaction of the condition of a production rule. The deletion of the data items a, b, c, need not be monitored since a conflict set that holds previously matched but not yet fired production rules does not exist. Therefore, the falsification of a previously satisfied declarative condition is indifferent.

Deductive rules. In the case of deductive rules, the monitoring of the deletion of condition items is required in order to keep the database consistent. For example, consider the following deductive rule:

$$D_1: \text{IF a \& b THEN d}$$

which is translated into the following 4 ECA rules:

```
ED₁: ON insert(a)  IF b THEN insert(d)
ED₂: ON insert(b)  IF a THEN insert(d)
ED₃: ON delete(a)  IF b THEN delete(d)
ED₄: ON delete(b)  IF a THEN delete(d)
```

where the event delete(x) monitors the deletion of the x data item.

Furthermore, the *delete-and-re-derive* approach of Ceri and Widom [35] requires one more rule to check and re-insert some deleted derived objects due to possible alternative derivations:

ED_5: ON delete(d) IF a & b THEN insert(d)

The approach of Griefahn and Manthey [72], on the other hand, avoids the unnecessary deletions in the first place by incorporating a check in the condition of the "deletion" rules about the alternative derivations:

ED'_3: ON delete(a) IF b & ¬d THEN delete(d)

Notice that the ¬d will be re-evaluated based on the deductive rule definition in the new state that the database has come after the deletion of d.

The Single-Rule Approach

The single-rule integration scheme is based on the compilation of the condition of the declarative rule into a discrimination network that is built from complex events. The complex event network is associated with the event-part of an ECA rule. In this way the condition of the declarative rule is constantly monitored by the active database. The condition-part of the ECA rule is usually missing, except in some cases that will be mentioned later. Finally, the action-part of the ECA rule depends on the type of the declarative rule.

This technique has been proposed for both production and deductive rules in [16, 17, 18]. In the next chapter we will present an in-depth analysis of this technique.

Production rules. Following the single-rule compilation scheme, the production rule P_1 is translated into the following ECA rule:

```
SP₁: ON    insert(a) & insert(b) & insert(c)
     [IF   true]
     THEN  <action>
```

where the operator & denotes the conjunction of the events.

The event manager of the ADB monitors individually the above primitive events. When each of them is detected its parameters are propagated and stored in the discrimination network, much alike the production systems (see the section *Data-driven Rules* of the previous chapter). When more than one of them are detected their parameters are combined at the nodes of the network in order to detect the occurrence of the complex event *incrementally*. When, finally, the complex event is detected, the condition of the rule has been matched and the event manager forwards a tuple (or token) with the complex event's parameters to the rule manager which is responsible to schedule it for execution.

Notice that the incremental condition matching requires that when a primitive event occurrence is detected, then its parameters must be matched against the parameters of all previously detected event occurrences for the rest of the events, rather than only with the currently occurred ones. In order to achieve this, the parameters of all event occurrences are kept in the complex event network even after the end of the transaction. Actually, they are never deleted unless an explicit deletion is issued. More details on the run-time behavior of the complex event network are described in the next chapter.

Deductive rules. Deductive rule compilation is more complex than production rules. However, for presentation purposes we initially assume that an equivalent compilation scheme suffices; therefore, the deductive rule D_1 is translated into the following ECA rule:

```
SD₁: ON    insert(a) & insert(b)
     [IF   true]
     THEN  insert(d)
```

The above rule only monitors the insertion of condition data items. However, their deletion must be monitored and catered for as well, as we explained above. The above ECA rule is, therefore, extended with an ELSE part which is executed when the condition of the original deductive rule is falsified due to the deletion of one or more of the data items:

```
SD'₁: ON    insert(a) & insert(b)
      [IF   true]
      THEN  insert(d)
      ELSE  delete(d)
```

Finally, a counting mechanism, that was introduced by Gupta et al. in [76], is used in order to check if the derived object that is about to be deleted has alternative derivations. The exact details of the translation of deductive rules are given in the next chapter.

Comparison

In the following, we analyze the disadvantages of the many-rule translation approach compared to the single-rule scheme.

Rule maintenance. In the multi-rule translation scheme, if someone wants to delete or temporarily disable a declarative rule, he/she must perform the same operation to all related ECA rules. However, this requires special care since the user might forget some of the ECA rules, and the rule base would then become inconsistent.

The single-rule approach avoids this problem by creating only one rule which is maintained more easily. The de-activation of all the events (both simple and complex ones) associated with a deleted or disabled rule is automatically done by the system.

Redundant condition checking. Recall the production rule P_1 and the equivalent, according to the multi-rule translation scheme, 3 ECA rules EP_1-EP_3. Assume that the ECA rules have immediate EC coupling modes. We will examine what happens when the following sequence of events occurs, in the same transaction, in an empty database:

$$\texttt{insert(c); insert(b); insert(a)}$$

ECA rules are considered in the following order: EP_3, EP_2, EP_1. First EP_3 and then EP_2 are triggered but not executed since their conditions are not satisfied. Finally EP_1 is triggered, its condition is satisfied, and the action is executed. This behavior is correct since the production rule P_1 should be fired after the insertion of c, b, a.

However, the above sequence of rule triggering creates performance problems since 3 ECA rules are triggered, and 6 condition elements are checked either successfully or not. Each of the 3 condition elements a, b, c is checked twice; the first time the check fails, while the second succeeds. This redundancy leads to poor performance, compared to the performance of the single-rule approach [17, 18] where each data item is checked only once.

Redundant action execution. Now re-consider the above event occurrence sequence but with the assumption that all 3 ECA rules have deferred EC coupling mode. This means that at the end of the transaction all the ECA rules are triggered and executed because the data items have already been inserted by the time the rule conditions are considered. However, all 3 rules will execute the same action. This creates a problem because it is incorrect.

Of course, various conflict resolution strategies and/or priorities can be established at compile-time or during the design of the ECA rule base, in order to prevent the redundant execution of multiple rule actions. However, this solution complicates things further because these conflict resolution strategies must be enforced separately from the semantical conflict resolution criteria.

The single-rule approach avoids this problem by having a single rule. Furthermore, the DEVICE system that will be presented in the next chapter has a centralized rule manager that resolves conflicts among multiple production rules, allowing only one to fire according to various semantical conflict resolution criteria.

Net effect. One more problem associated with the immediate EC coupling mode is the absence of the *net effect* of events. When an event triggers a rule and that rule is selected for execution, there is no way to "undo" the rule activation by reversing the effect of the triggering event. For example, when the creation of the object activates a rule, the rule is going to fire even if the object is deleted before the end of the transaction.

This problem exists for the rules with immediate EC coupling, even if the underlying active system does support net effects, because rules are immediately activated without waiting for the end of the transaction. The immediate mode is simply not compatible with the state description nature of declarative rule conditions.

One way to overcome the absence of net effects, in the case of immediate EC and deferred CA coupling modes, is to re-check the condition inside the action of the ECA rule in order to assure that the event and the condition that triggered the rule after the event signaling is still true at the end of the transaction. For example rule EP_1 would look under this scheme as follows[2]:

```
ON insert(a) IF b & c THEN (a&b&c → <action>; true)
```

In the case of deferred EC and CA coupling, the check should be included only in the condition:

```
ON insert(a) IF a & b & c THEN <action>
```

However, the above solution would incur overhead on the performance of rule execution because it duplicates checking of already checked conditions. The single-rule approach avoids this problem of net event effects by delaying the execution of triggered rules until the end of the transaction.

---

[2] The notation (a→b;c) is the notation of Prolog for the usual *if-then-else* programming construct and it means *"if a (is true) then (execute) b else (execute) c"*.

4 AN ACTIVE OBJECT-ORIENTED KNOWLEDGE BASE SYSTEM

In the previous chapter we have presented various techniques for unifying two or more different rule paradigms. Among the techniques presented was the single-rule translation scheme which integrates production and deductive rules into an active database system that generically supports only ECA rules. In this chapter, we present in detail an active object-oriented knowledge base system, called DEVICE [16, 17, 18], which uses the single-rule translation approach.

In the following, we first describe the architecture and the rule language of the DEVICE system. Then the operational semantics of declarative rules in DEVICE are described along with their integration with event-driven rules. The details of compiling the declarative rule conditions into complex event networks are presented separately in order to make clear how rule conditions are incrementally matched at run-time. Finally, optimization and extensibility issues of the system are discussed.

The System Architecture

The overall architecture of the DEVICE system is shown in Figure 2. DEVICE mainly consists of classes and meta-classes which are introduced to the core active OODB system and extend its functionality. More specifically, DEVICE consists of two major components: compile-time and run-time modules.

The compile-time modules of DEVICE are mainly meta-classes that host the methods for generating declarative rules. This includes a) a parser, which parses the textual description of the rule and, furthermore, applies a series of transformations to

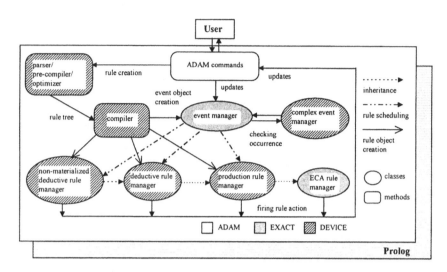

Figure 2. The architecture of the DEVICE system

the parse tree in order to produce a more efficient and easy to compile tree (pre-compiler/optimizer), and b) a compiler which compiles the parse tree into a network of complex events and one ECA rule using the single-rule translation technique we described in the previous chapter.

The run-time modules of DEVICE are various OODB classes that host the structure and behavior of complex events, production and deductive rules, etc. They are usually referred to as *managers*, such as the complex event manager, the production rule manager, etc. Rules and events are first-class objects, instances of the corresponding managers. Managers themselves are instances of the meta-classes we have described above.

The ECA rule manager is the most generic rule manager and is part of the core active OODB system. The various rule managers that implement the functionality of DEVICE are subclasses of the ECA rule manager which means that they inherit part of the functions of the generic rule manager while they re-define many of them in order to capture the higher-level semantics of production and deductive rules.

In addition, new types of events (complex events) have been introduced as subtypes of the generic OODB events. These are fixed, and they are the building components of the complex event discrimination network that is used to match the declarative rules' conditions. The event manager keeps track of which simple events have occurred and combines them incrementally to match the rules' conditions.

The DEVICE system is fully implemented on top of ECLiPSe Prolog as an extension to the active OODB EXACT [56], which is itself an extension of ADAM OODB [109]. The various components are plugged-in as modules, extending the basic active OODB system, rather than being placed on a distinct layer on top of the EXACT and ADAM systems. This is a consequence of the OODB extensibility through meta-classes [112] and makes DEVICE itself extensible. At the end of this chapter we present more details on the extensibility of DEVICE.

The Rule Language

This section describes the system's declarative rule language which follows, for the most part, the OPS5 [59] paradigm influenced by the OODB context of DEVICE. Both types of declarative rules which are supported by DEVICE are expressed as a *condition* which defines a pattern of objects to be detected over the database, followed by a *consequent* which takes the form of an *action* (for production rules) or a *conclusion* (for deductive rules). The language for defining low-level ECA rules is described in [56, 57].

Rule Condition

The condition of a rule is an *inter-object* pattern which consists of the conjunction of one or more (positive or negative) *intra-object* patterns. The intra-object patterns consist of one or more *attribute* patterns. For example, the following rule condition defines an employee working in the 'Security' department but his/her manager is different from the department's manager:

```
PR₁: IF     E@emp(dept:D,manager:M) and
            D@dept(name='Security',manager\=M)
       THEN  delete ⇒ E
```

The first of the above intra-object patterns denotes an instance E of class emp. The second intra-object pattern describes the department D of employee E whose name attribute is equal to 'Security' and its manager attribute is different from the manager M of E.

Variables in front of the class names denote instances of the class. Inside the brackets, attribute patterns are denoted by relational comparisons, either directly with constants or indirectly through variables. Variables are also used to deliver values for comparison to other intra-object patterns (joins) in the same condition or to the action part of the rule. The values can be both object references and normal values, e.g. integers, strings.

We notice here that the condition of PR_1 can be written also as:

```
E@emp(name.dept='Security',manager:M,manager.dept\=M)
```

Attribute patterns can navigate through object references of complex attributes, such as the complex attribute `name.dept`. The innermost attribute should be an attribute of class `emp`. Moving from right to the left of the expression, attributes belong to classes related through object-reference attributes of the class of their predecessor attributes. We have adopted a right-to-left order of attributes, contrary to the C-like dot notation that is commonly assumed because we would like to stress the functional data model origins of ADAM [71]. Under this interpretation, the chained "dotted" attributes can be seen as function compositions.

During a pre-compilation phase, each rule that contains complex attribute expressions is transformed into one that contains only simple attribute expressions by introducing new intra-object patterns. The above pattern is actually transformed into the condition of PR_1.

There can also be negated intra-object patterns in the condition[3]. A negated intra-object pattern denotes a negative condition that is satisfied when no objects in the database satisfy the corresponding positive intra-object pattern. The following rule condition identifies an employee who has worked more hours than anyone.

```
PR₂: IF    E1@emp(hours_worked:H,salary:S) and
           not E2@emp(hours_worked>H) and
           prolog{S1 is 1.1*S}
     THEN  update_salary([S,S1]) ⇒ E1
```

The use of arbitrary Prolog or ADAM goals to express some small static conditions or to compute certain values is allowed in the condition through the special `prolog{}` construct. In appendix A, we include the full syntax of the condition-part language.

Rule Consequent

The rule consequent differs for each different rule type. In this chapter we present two types of rule consequents, namely production rule actions and deductive rule conclusions. In [18] rule consequents for other rule types can be found.

Production rule actions. The action part of a production rule defines a set of updates to be performed on the database objects that were identified in the rule condition. These updates are expressed in an extended Prolog language which

---

[3] Only safe rules are allowed.

includes the default procedural data manipulation language of ADAM. The syntax of the ADAM messages can be found in [71].

Examples of production rule actions are given in rules PR_1 and PR_2 above. In PR_1, a 'Security' employee is deleted when his/her manager is different from the departments manager whereas, in PR_2, the harder worker's salary is increased by 10%.

Deductive rule conclusion. Deductive rules have a *conclusion* instead of an action. The conclusion is a *derived class template* that defines the objects that are derivable when the condition is true.

```
DR₁: IF     E@emp(name:N,name.manager:M)
     THEN   manages(supervisor:M,subordinate:N)
DR₂: IF     M1@manages(supervisor:M,subordinate:X) and
            E@emp(name:N,name.manager:X)
     THEN   manages(supervisor:M,subordinate:N)
```

The deductive rule DR_1 defines that an object with attributes supervisor, subordinate is an instance of class manages if there is an employee E named N in class emp with attribute manager equal to M.

Class manages is a derived class, i.e. a class whose instances are derived from deductive rules. Only one derived class template is allowed at the *head* of a deductive rule. However, there can exist many rules with the same derived class at the head. The final set of the derived objects is a union of objects derived by all the rules that define the derived class. For example, the transitive closure of the supervisor-subordinate relation is completed with the recursive rule DR_2.

The derived class template consists of attribute-value pairs where the value can either be a variable that appears in the condition or a constant. The syntax is given in appendix A.

Integration of Declarative Rules

The declarative rules that were described in the previous section are integrated in the active database system following these steps:

1. The condition of the rule is compiled into a discrimination network that consists of complex events;

2. The last event in the network is the triggering event of the ECA rule;

3.   The condition part of the ECA rule is usually *true* because all condition tests have been incorporated into the complex event. However, if the `prolog{}` construct is present, then the Prolog goals are incorporated in the condition of the ECA rule;

4.   The action part of the ECA rule depends on the declarative rule type. Production rule actions are directly copied to the ECA rule action, while deductive rules need a more complex treatment. There is actually an action and an anti-action part for deductive/ECA rules that insert/delete a derived object, respectively.

At run-time, the active database system monitors the simple events that have been created for the declarative rules. When a simple event is detected it is signaled to the event manager who is responsible for propagating it, along with its parameters, to the complex event network. The parameters of either simple and complex events are propagated through tokens which are tuples that constitute of condition variables and their values.

Tokens can be positive or negative depending on the initial simple insertion or deletion event that has been detected. If a token is propagated through the whole complex event network, it means that the corresponding rule has been either matched (in the case of positive tokens) or unmatched (in the case of negative tokens). The rule along with the last event's parameters is called rule instantiation, and is forwarded to the appropriate rule manager in order to schedule it for execution.

In the rest of this section we describe in more detail the semantics of production and deductive rule integration in DEVICE.

Production Rules

The production rule manager receives all the detected complex event occurrences from the event manager and selects those events that activate production rules. The positive rule instantiation tokens are placed into the "conflict set". The negative tokens cause the corresponding positive rule instantiations to be removed from the conflict set, if they still exist there.

When multiple rule instantiations are placed in the conflict set, there is an ambiguity concerning the number and order of rules to be executed. The OPS5 approach applies heuristic strategies to select a unique rule instantiation to execute [59]. The active database systems' approach uses priorities to resolve the rule execution order. In DEVICE, the OPS5 conflict resolution heuristics have been incorporated into the priority mechanism of the active OODB system. The application of any of the heuristics is controlled by an appropriate class variable of the rule manager that can be set to on or off.

The conflict set is a Prolog list (LIFO structure) that is stored as a class attribute in the production rule manager. The *refractoriness* criteria removes the rule instantiation tokens that have been executed from the conflict list. The *recency* criteria inserts the newly derived rule instantiations at the beginning of the conflict list, in order to be considered before the older ones.

Finally, the *specificity* criteria selectively picks-up at run-time from the conflict set rule instantiation tokens that their conditions are more specific than the others. The specificity of a rule is determined by the number of event objects involved during condition matching and is calculated at compile-time by counting the total number of generated events for the condition. Notice that because the specificity of a rule is based on the number of actually generated events and not on the syntactical complexity of its condition, deep path expressions in the condition may produce a high specificity score that is at first not comprehensible from the simple high-level rule declaration.

The specificity heuristic has been blended with the rule priority mechanism of EXACT. The specificity of each rule is used by the system at rule-creation time to place the rule (not the rule instantiation) into a partially ordered set, called `ordered_rule_list`, which keeps the OIDs for each production rule object. The DEVICE mechanism instead of storing the totally ordered rule instantiation set in the conflict list, it dynamically creates it at selection time by intersecting the conflict list with the `ordered_rule_list`. The first rule instantiation in the above set is selected for execution.

After the rule manager selects a rule instantiation for execution, the condition part of the rule is checked. Usually the trivial `true` condition is associated with DEVICE rules unless the `prolog{}` construct is present at the rule definition. If the condition evaluates to false, then the rule is not fired. If the condition is confirmed, then the action part of the rule must be scheduled for execution. The action is executed as a compound Prolog goal using the immediate CA coupling mode.

In DEVICE, rule selection and execution are initiated either at the end of the transaction or at intermediate user-specified *checkpoints*. After the first rule instantiation is selected and executed, the rule manager self-raises a checkpoint in order to continue with the next production cycle by considering all the previous rule instantiations plus any new ones that have been produced by the execution of rule actions. This cycle continues until a *fixpoint* is reached where there are no more rule instantiations left in the conflict set. This happens when rule actions either do not produce new rule instantiations or evoke explicit object deletions that propagate up to the conflict set. After the fixpoint is reached, the control of the transaction is given back to the user.

The *net effect* of events is guaranteed by the deferred EC coupling mode. When two events of the same transaction cause contradictory (a positive and a negative) rule instantiation placements in the conflict set, then the rule instantiation is eliminated from the conflict set before the rule selection and execution sequences begin at the end of the transaction. Therefore, no rule is executed. When the two events above are issued at different transactions but the rule instantiation in question has not yet been selected for execution, a similar net effect is produced.

Deductive Rules

The integration of both materialized and non-materialized deductive rules, in DEVICE, is achieved by mapping the deductive rule semantics on production rules (see the section *Unification of Production and Deductive Rule Semantics* of the previous chapter).

As it was noticed in the previous chapter the simple production rule translation scheme is not adequate to fully capture the semantics of deductive rules. There are certain extensions that should be made: a) the anti-action or ELSE part, and b) the counting mechanism.

In order to model the deletion of a derived object, production rules are extended with an `anti_action` (or ELSE) part that hosts the derived object deletion algorithm. Using this extended scheme, a deductive rule can be modeled by a single production rule if the positive action is mapped to the `action` part of the rule, and the negative action is mapped to the `anti_action` part:

```
IF     condition
THEN   create(object))
ELSE   delete(object))
```

Furthermore, the rule manager should be extended in order to be able to execute the anti-action rule part upon the receipt of a negative token from the event manager. Therefore, the semantics of deductive rules are implemented under a new deductive rule manager that is a subclass of the production rule manager. The former inherits a part of the common behavior from the latter and overrides some of the structural and behavioral features of the latter.

Concerning the multiple derivations problem, before a derived object is removed from the database it must be ensured that it is not deducible by another rule instantiation. For this reason, a counter mechanism which stores the number of derivations of an object [76] is used. If the derived object has a counter equal to 1, then it is deleted; otherwise the counter is only decreased by 1.

Furthermore, the creation of a new derived object should only be done if the object does not already exist, otherwise two distinct objects with the same attribute values will exist. This is a consequence of the generic differences between the OID-based OODBs and the value-based deductive databases [139]. When a derived object already exists, then its counter is just increased by 1.

The above operational semantics is modeled by the following extended production rule which is translated into an ECA rule using the procedure described at the beginning of this section:

```
IF    condition
THEN  (exists(object)  →    inc_counter(object);
                            create(object))
ELSE  (counter(object)>1 →  dec_counter(object);
                            delete(object))
```

The conflict resolution strategies of deductive rules differ from production rules. The recency strategy is not used and, therefore, new rule instantiations are appended to the conflict set. The rule search space is, thus, navigated in a breadth-first manner in order to model the set-oriented semi-naive evaluation of deductive rules [138].

Specificity is overridden by the *stratification* control strategy. When a deductive rule is created, the derived classes that appear in the condition are collected along with their strata. The algorithm presented in Ullman [138] checks if the new rule, along with the existing ones, constitute a stratified logic program and modifies their strata as a side-effect. The strata define a partial ordering of rules which is used to resolve rule selection at run-time using exactly the same algorithm as for specificity.

Non-materialized deductive rules. In this case, derived data is not permanently stored in the database but is computed only as needed as a response to given queries. Non-materialized deductive rules are a special case of the materialized ones and are compiled normally but not activated. Thus, the associated primitive events are not detected by the event manager and, consequently, not propagated to the event network.

When a query about a derived class is made, two ECA rules, signaled before and after the query, are executed. The first rule gathers all the non-materialized derived classes from the dependency graph that contribute to the derivation of the queried derived class and activates all their associated rules. This causes the retrospective detection of primitive events and the propagation of their parameters to the event network. Finally, the selected rules are executed using the default mechanism for deductive rules and temporarily materialize the derived objects. After the query is executed, the second active rule de-activates all the rules and deletes the derived objects.

Certain optimizations of the non-materialized approach, such as magic sets, can be introduced to limit the number of derived objects to just the necessary to answer to a given query. This approach, of course, has the overhead of compilation and can be used only for large databases and computations. An alternative solution would be to precompile parameterized transformed rule sets using every alternative goal adornment.

Condition Compilation and Matching

The efficient matching of production rule conditions is usually achieved through a discrimination network. DEVICE smoothly integrates a RETE-like discrimination network into an active OODB system as a set of first class objects by mapping each node of the network onto a complex event object of the ADB system. This section overviews both the structure and behavior of the network along with the compilation process that produces it. More details about both the compilation and run-time aspects of the network nodes can be found in [16, 17].

Structure and Behavior of the Complex Event Network

The complex event network consists of 3 event types: primitive, logical, and two-input events. Throughout this section, we describe the structure and behavior of these event types using the following example:

```
DR'₁: IF      E@emp(name:N,name.manager:'Nick')
      THEN    manages(supervisor:'Nick',subordinate:N)
DR'₂: IF      M1@manages(supervisor:'Nick',subordinate:X)
              and E@emp(name:N,name.manager:X)
      THEN    manages(supervisor:'Nick',subordinate:N)
```

It is obvious that the example is derived from rules DR_1 and DR_2 of previous sections. However, the new rules do not compute all the derivable manages objects but only those that indicate the subordinates of a certain employee. The complex event network for rule DR'₂ is shown in Figure 3.

Primitive events. The DEVICE network has multiple input sources which are the primitive database events detected by the active database system. Each attribute pattern inside any intra-object pattern in the condition is mapped on a primitive event that monitors the insertion (or deletion) of values at the corresponding attribute. In Figure 3, there are several primitive events, such as put_supervisor, put_subordinate, etc., and their delete_ type counterparts.

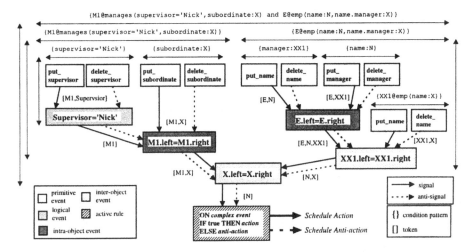

Figure 3. A sample complex event network

The creation of whole database objects could be monitored by the event new of the class of the intra-object patterns. However, method new iterates over the attributes of the newly created object and inserts them using the default put_ type methods. Hence, the monitoring of primitive put_ type events suffice and is more flexible since it can capture simple attribute updates. Similar arguments also hold for the deletion of objects and the corresponding delete_ type events. Actually, this is an optimization of the compilation that is specific only to EXACT/ADAM. Other extensible OODB systems might require also the monitoring of the object creation event new.

The *signaling* of a put_ type primitive event denotes that a certain database state has been reached by inserting data in the database. On the other hand, the occurrence of delete_ type events denotes that a certain pattern in the rule condition that was previously present in the database is no longer valid. To model such semantics, *anti-signaling* is used. We notice that update_ type events are emulated by anti-signaling a delete_ type event followed by the signaling of a put_ type event.

When primitive events are signaled (or anti-signaled), the event manager forwards a positive (or negative) token with the message parameters to the successor network nodes via the corresponding checking (anti_checking) method. These methods internally process the input tokens and check if a complex event can be signaled according to the current input signal and the local history of event activation. When appropriate, these methods construct output tokens that are forwarded further in the event network.

Logical events. Logical events perform simple attribute tests, and they are only raised when the associated condition is satisfied. In DEVICE, logical events map attribute comparisons with constants, and they are signaled by primitive events to perform a check on their parameter. If the check is successful, an output token is propagated to a successor event in the event network. Logical events are the equivalent of α-memories of the RETE network. In Figure 3, there is one such logical event for the attribute test against the constant 'Nick'.

Two-input events. An intra-object pattern that consists of at least two attribute patterns is translated into a two-input event (also called *intra-object event*) that joins the parameters of the input events (primitive and/or logical) based on the OID the message recipient objects. In Figure 3, there are two intra-object events even if there are three intra-object patterns in the condition of rule DR'$_2$. This happens because the hidden intra-object pattern that the complex attribute is analyzed into has only one attribute pattern.

When an intra-object pattern consists of more than two attribute patterns, then the intra-object event that joins the first two attribute patterns is further joined with the remaining attribute patterns into new intra-object events and so on and so forth until all the attribute patterns are catered for.

Multiple intra-object patterns are mapped into multiple intra-object events that are joined in pairs based on the shared variables between the intra-object patterns in the rule condition. These events are called *inter-object events*. In Figure 3, there are two inter-object events: the first joins the two intra-object patterns on the value of variable X, while the second is a consequence of the complex attribute.

The last inter-object event of the network maps the whole rule condition, and it is directly attached to the ECA rule that maps the original rule.

Intra-object and inter-object events are collectively called two-input events and are treated in a uniform way. Here they have been analyzed separately for mere presentation purposes. Two-input events are the equivalent of β-memories of the RETE network.

Two-input events receive tokens from both inputs whose behavior is symmetrical. The positive incoming tokens are permanently stored at the corresponding input memories and are joined with the tokens of the opposite memory. The join produces one or more positive output tokens according to a pre-compiled pattern and are propagated further to the event network.

For example, in Figure 3, assume that there exist 2 employees in the database that are directly managed by the employee 'Nick'. Both of them will cause the creation of two manages objects, due to rule DR'$_1$. These two manages objects correspond to tokens that reside at the left memory of the two-input inter-object event, e.g.:

```
[11#manages,'Jack'], [22#manages,'John']
```

The name of the supervisor ('Nick') is not stored in the tokens because the condition pattern merely tests it. Therefore, it is not forwarded beyond the corresponding logical event.

The two original emp objects are also stored as tokens in the right memory of the last inter-object event:

```
['Jack','Nick'], ['John','Nick']
```

If a new emp object, subordinate of 'Jack', is inserted in the database, then the token, e.g.:

```
['George','Jack']
```

is signaled at the right input, stored at the right memory, and joined with the above two tokens of the left memory. The join succeeds only for the first token; therefore, the token ['George'] is signaled at the output of the two-input event to indicate that 'George' is a new subordinate of 'Nick'.

Token deletion. Tokens describe database states, and they persist inside the two-input event memories beyond the end of the transaction. They can be only explicitly deleted to reflect deletions in the database. The deletion of tokens is triggered by the propagation of anti-signals in the network.

When a two-input event receives a negative token at one of its inputs, it deletes it from the corresponding memory and a negative token is output from the event. The output token contains elements only from the deleted (incomplete) token because there is no need to join it with the tokens of the right memory. This deletion optimization [77] is valid because the tokens that flow among two-input events contain the unique OIDs of the objects involved in the condition. Therefore, there can be no ambiguity concerning the matching of incomplete tokens. Furthermore, when an incomplete token arrives at an input node, it is matched against the stored full tokens of the corresponding memory. Therefore, the output token is more informative that the input one because it contains more variables.

For example, consider rule DR$_2$ (not DR'$_2$). In addition, assume that the tokens of the previous example still exist at the memories of the two-input events. If the following message:

```
delete_name(['George']) ⇒ 41#emp
```

is sent, then the negative token:

```
[41#emp,'George']
```

is propagated to the left input of the intra-object event for class emp. There, it is matched with the stored tokens (only one match), deleted from the left memory, and an incomplete negative token:

```
[41#emp,'George',XX1]
```

is propagated to the left input of the inter-object event that is due to the complex-attribute.

Again, it is matched with the stored tokens and deleted, and the incomplete negative token:

```
['George',X]
```

is output to the right-input of the last inter-object event. In the right-input, it is matched with the stored tokens, variable X is instantiated to 'Jack', and the token is deleted from the right-input memory. Finally, the incomplete token:

```
[M,'George']
```

is propagated to the deductive rule manager which "requests" the deletion of the partially instantiated derived object:

```
manages(supervisor:M,subordinate:'George')
```

This partial instantiation is interpreted as *"delete all manages objects that have George as their subordinate"* which is not correct because their might be other employees named 'George'; therefore, only the manages objects that depend on the 41#emp object should be deleted.

The last example shows that the only two-input event that is not entitled to deletion optimization is the last one of the network since the action or the conclusion of the rule might "project away" some of the OID (or other) variables. Consequently, the propagation of the "deletion" from the condition to the action is non-deterministic.

Practically, the execution or non-execution of the join is controlled by the presence of a rule object at the output of a two-input event. When the event outputs to a rule, then the join is performed. Otherwise the deletion optimization holds, and incomplete tokens are output.

Negation. Negative intra-object patterns denote conditions that should not be met in order for the whole rule condition to become true. The negative patterns are treated much the same as the positive ones, and they are mapped into one or more chained intra-object events (two-input events) that correspond to the equivalent positive patterns. The first inter-object event, however, that is connected to the last node of the intra-object event that corresponds to the negative pattern behaves in a slightly different manner than a usual (positive) inter-object event. Such a two-input event that one of its input nodes maps a negative condition element is called a *negative event*.

For instance, consider the following rule that derives the highest paid employee in each department:

```
DR₃:  IF    El@emp(dept:D,salary:S) and
            not E2@emp(dept:D,salary>S)
       THEN put_highest_paid_employee([El]) ⇒ D
```

The negative condition pattern causes a normal intra-object event that corresponds to the positive pattern to be created. However, the inter-object event that connects the two intra-object events is not a normal, positive two-input event, but rather a negative one because its right input stems from a negative condition pattern (Figure 4).

Structurally, positive and negative events do not differ. However, their behavior is different because the detection of the intra-object event at the negative input indicates that the (negative) inter-object event does not occur and vice-versa. Another difference between positive and negative events is that the former have symmetrical inputs, i.e. the algorithms are the same regardless of the input source. Negative events, however, behave differently depending on the input source: the "negative" or the "positive" inputs. The "negative" input does not contribute values

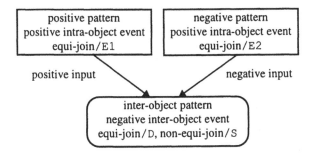

Figure 4. A negative event example

to the output token of the inter-object event because the negation is not constructive and only stands for value testing (safety requirement).

This is the reason why two negative intra-object events are never joined into an inter-object event. If this were done, no tokens would be propagated by the latter. Instead, the pre-compilation phase ensures that the order of intra-object patterns in the rule condition are such that a negative pattern is always joined with a positive one. More specifically, the complex event network is constructed in such a manner, that the "left" input of a negative event is always the "positive" input while the "right" input is the "negative" one.

When a negative event receives a positive token from its "positive" input and the input token does not match with any tokens stored at the "negative" memory, then a positive token is output. Otherwise nothing happens.

For instance, if the tokens:

```
[39#emp,1#dept,500000],  [11#emp,2#dept,250000]
```

are stored at the right memory of the negative event and the token:

```
[48#emp,3#dept,370000]
```

arrives at the positive input, it does not match with any of the previous tokens, and the positive token [3#dept] is output. On the other hand, if the token:

```
[96#emp,2#dept,450000]
```

arrives at the positive input, then it matches with the token

```
[39#emp,1#dept,500000]
```

and no output token is propagated.

When the "negative" input receives a positive token which matches some of the tokens stored at the "positive" memory, negative tokens are output. Of course, the negative tokens may not correspond to past positive tokens, but this check is left out for optimization reasons, unless the negative event directly outputs to a declarative rule. When these "unverified" negative tokens are received by a successive event in the network and they are not found at the corresponding memory, they are just ignored. When no match exists for the input token, nothing happens.

For instance, if the tokens:

```
[48#emp,3#dept,370000], [96#emp,2#dept,450000]
```

are stored at the left memory of the negative event and the positive token:

```
[11#emp,2#dept,250000]
```

arrives at the negative input then it does not match with any of the previous tokens and no output token is propagated. On the other hand, if the positive token:

```
[69#emp,2#dept,500000]
```

arrives at the negative input, it matches with the token

```
[96#emp,2#dept,450000]
```

and the negative token [2#dept] is output.

Finally, when a negative event receives a negative token from its "positive" input, the behavior is exactly the same as with the behavior of a positive event. However, when the negative token arrives at the "negative" input, the behavior is pretty much complicated. Specifically, if the input token matches some tokens of the "positive" memory, these are candidate output tokens. The latter are again matched against the "negative" memory. This is done in case of non-equijoins where a single token can match more than one tokens of the opposite memory. The candidate output tokens that do not match any tokens of the "negative" memory are finally forwarded as positive output tokens.

For instance, if the token:

```
[96#emp,2#dept,450000]
```

is stored at the left memory of the negative event, the tokens:

```
[29#emp,2#dept,550000], [39#emp,2#dept,580000]
```

are stored at the right memory and the negative token:

```
[29#emp,2#dept,550000]
```

arrives at the negative input, it matches with the token:

```
[96#emp,2#dept,450000]
```

of the left memory, and the latter is a candidate positive output token. However, 96#emp is still not the employee with the highest salary in department 2#dept because there is one more employee (39#emp) whose salary is larger.

If the candidate token of the left memory is re-matched with the tokens of the "negative" memory, it is found that it cannot be propagated at the output because it matches with at least one token ([39#emp,2#dept,580000]) of the "negative" memory. Therefore, this candidate token is rejected, and since there is no other candidate, no tokens are output.

The Compilation Process

The compilation process consists of 3 phases. During phase-1 (precompilation), the rule is parsed; the complex attribute references are transformed to simple attributes in multiple intra-object patterns; and the parse tree is optimized through re-ordering (see next section).

The main compilation phase consists of 2 stages. During stage-1, the condition is scanned in order to identify and create the primitive and logical events needed to monitor all the attribute patterns of the condition. This stage also collects information to assist stage-2 about the variables of the condition and action. During stage-2, the primitive and logical events are joined in pairs to form two-input events, based on the common variables. First the intra-object and then the inter-object events are constructed.

Finally, in phase-3, the ECA rule is created and linked with the last event of the discrimination network. After rule creation, the rule is activated by recursively propagating activation messages down to the primitive events. The latter query the database for objects that already exist and signal the tokens upwards to the network as if the objects were inserted now to an empty database. In this way, the network is correctly initialized with information about pre-existing data.

Optimization and Extensibility

In this section we describe various implementation optimizations in order to reduce the time and space complexity of rule condition matching. Furthermore, we outline the process under which DEVICE can be extended with new rule types.

Storage Optimization

The event network requires a large storage space for the two-input memories and can duplicate the contents of the database in certain cases. In order to avoid such a waste of space, DEVICE has introduced certain optimizations to the basic discrimination network that require less space at no or very little extra performance cost. These are the virtual and hybrid memories of two-input events.

Virtual memories. Virtual memories save storage space for rule conditions that include attribute patterns with no attribute tests. This optimization also increases the performance of matching since the storage management of large event memories requires some extra time that is not compensated by the smaller size of the joined relations because there is no selection associated with the node. Consider for example the following intra-object pattern:

```
E@emp(name='John',salary:S)
```

There is not a direct test associated with attribute `salary`; therefore, nothing is gained by storing all the signaled `[E,S]` tokens at the corresponding intra-object event memory. Instead, the values of the attribute `salary` are directly retrieved from the original `emp` objects when required with no performance penalty.

The same principle applies to larger patterns of the condition as well:

```
M1@manages(supervisor:M,subordinate:X) and
E@emp(name:N,name.manager:X)
```

Both (or rather all three) intra-object patterns consist of attribute patterns with no direct attribute tests. There is no gain if all signaled tokens are stored at the memories of the successor inter-object event. Instead, the values of the attributes are directly retrieved from the database objects when required. In this example, none of the variables are stored. Therefore, there is 100% saving in storage space of two-input memories. Virtual memories can appear only at intra-object events or at the first successor inter-object event.

Hybrid memories. Hybrid memories mix stored and virtual variable values in an input token of an inter-object event. Hybrid memories store only the absolutely necessary information and retrieve the rest of the token values from the original database objects. Consider the following rule condition:

```
E1@emp(name='John',age:A1,salary:S) and
E2@emp(hours_worked>160,age:A,salary=S) and
E3@emp(name.dept='Security',age=A,salary:S3>500000) and
prolog{Avg is (A1+2*A2)/3, Avg > 30}
```

This condition involves 3 related instances of class `emp` with various differing selection criteria. When each of the 3 intra-object events emanates an output token, it means that a certain `emp` object has satisfied the corresponding intra-object pattern. This `emp` instance is uniquely identified by its OID; therefore, there is no need to

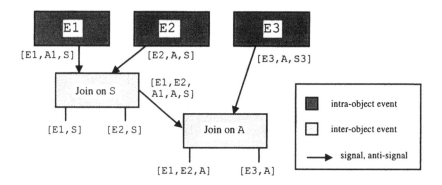

Figure 5. Hybrid memories of inter-object events

store in the input memories of the subsequent inter-object events the rest of the variables that appear inside the pattern because these can be very easily retrieved later by accessing the original object.

The above concept is illustrated in Figure 5. This shows that tokens flowing from event to event are different from the tokens actually stored in the corresponding memories. In addition to the OID variables that are stored in every memory, the join variable of each inter-object event is also stored at the input memories, in order to ease the process of joining at the expense of a little extra storage space at each memory. The rest of the variables that flow into each inter-object event are virtual, i.e. they are not stored but directly accessed via messages from the corresponding objects. A non-OID variable can become both a stored and a virtual variable, depending on the inter-object event, whereas OID variables are always stored variables.

At run-time, first the stored variables are matched against the incoming token and upon success the virtual variables are retrieved and matched. Of course, this extra complication of token retrieval and matching has some extra overhead because direct object access requires one message per attribute to be sent to the corresponding object while tokens are matched in one step. However, the gain in storage requirements can be much more significant. Specifically, for the above condition, only 9 out of 14 variables are stored in the inter-object memory space.

Join Optimization

The compiler of DEVICE iterates the parse tree produced by the parser in a left-to-right manner and creates the two-input events according to the shared variables. However, when the same variable is joined more than once then there is a question regarding which is the best way to order the joins to obtain the best complexity for the matching algorithm. Optimization of join plans is usually achieved through the use of statistical information about a certain database, e.g. relation sizes, existence of indices, etc.

In DEVICE we did not have such information handy; therefore, a more general purpose optimizer was used based on the most important principles of query optimization [114]. The optimizer of DEVICE transforms the parse tree that is produced from the parser (and the pre-compiler) into a tree that is likely to produce a less complex event network. The rules of transformation follow.

Push attribute tests as early as possible. Inside an intra-object pattern there may exist attribute patterns with or without tests. The latter lead to the creation of logical events that cut down the number of tokens flowing into the rest of the network. Such logical events should be placed as "left" as possible in the complex event network in order to reduce the cardinality of the joins for the intra-object events. Consider the following example:

```
E@emp(name:N, salary:S, age<35)
```

This intra-object pattern corresponds to two intra-object events of the event network; the first joins the tokens from the two primitive events `put_name`, `put_salary`, while the second joins the output token of the previous two-input event with the tokens of the logical event that checks the value of the attribute `age`. If the join is produced with this order then too many unnecessary name and salary values will be kept (and joined) at the first two-input event and at the left input of the second two-input event. The optimizer re-orders the above pattern into the following one that cuts down the number of joins and stored tokens at both two-input events.

```
E@emp(age<35, name:N, salary:S)
```

When multiple tests exist inside an intra-object pattern, then equalities are preferred to in-equalities and pushed as much to the left as possible.

Push selective conditions as early as possible. Based on the previous attribute test heuristic, each intra-object pattern is scored according to the total number of attribute tests it contains. Equalities count for 100 units, while inequalities for 1. This score is used to sort the intra-object patterns in the parse tree in descending order because a more selective condition element (with more tests) should be placed earlier in the join tree to produce a less complex run-time matching process.

For example, the following rule condition produces an event network with high complexity because the first intra-object event would allow many tokens to flow into the network; therefore, the cardinalities of the intermediate joins would be high.

```
E1@emp(name\='John', salary=S) and
```

```
E2@emp(name='John', salary=S) and
E3@emp(name='Nick', age>25&<35, salary:S)
```

The optimizer re-orders the above condition into the following one based on the attribute test scoring of each intra-object pattern.

```
E3@emp(name='Nick', age<35, salary:S) and
E2@emp(name='John', salary=S) and
E1@emp(name\='John', salary=S)
```

Extensibility

It is quite easy to extend DEVICE due to the following reasons:

- the OO architecture allows the transparent modification of existing system components or the introduction of new ones;

- the rule managers of DEVICE allow the modification of the rule semantics by changing the values of certain class attributes.

Deductive rules are an example of extending the basic DEVICE system. Furthermore, the integration of rules for derived and aggregate attributes has been presented in [18]. A new rule type is added in DEVICE by introducing two meta-classes: the rule manager and the rule manager's meta-class.

Rule manager. A new rule manager should be added as a subclass (direct or indirect) of the production rule manager (Figure 2). This gives the new rule manager inheritance of the default production rule semantics, such as the sharing of a common rule conflict set, the re-configurable conflict resolution criteria, and the rule action execution.

The conflict resolution criteria can be controlled by the corresponding class variables of the conflict set which can have on or off as their values. For example, the production and deductive rule managers have different conflict resolution criteria.

When two rule types have a direct type-subtype relationship and exactly the same conflict resolution criteria, they can share a common conflict set. This sharing is controlled by an attribute of the corresponding rule manager. If the sharing attribute is set to no, the rule manager has an independent conflict set from its super-type(s) and is activated individually by the rule scheduler. When this variable is set to yes, the rule manager shares the conflict set of its first super-class that has its sharing attribute set to no.

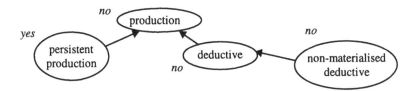

Figure 6. Sharing of conflict sets among the rule managers of DEVICE

The existing rule managers of DEVICE are shown in Figure 6. The rule manager of persistent production rules shares the conflict set of the volatile production rules while deductive and non-materialized deductive rules maintain their own conflict set.

Rule manager meta-class. The new rule manager can be either an instance of the meta-class of the production rule manager or a new meta-class can be generated as a subclass of the meta-class of the production rule manager. The former solution gives the new rule type a rule creation semantics (parsing, pre-compilation, optimization, compilation, rule object generation, etc.) similar to the one of production rules. The latter solution can be used when the new rule type partially inherits the rule generation semantics of production rules and partially re-defines them, as it is the case for deductive rules.

PART II PARALLEL DATABASE AND KNOWLEDGE BASE SYSTEMS

In this part of the book, we discuss issues concerning parallel database and knowledge base systems. Since knowledge base systems are database systems extended with a rule language, parallel databases are the core for building a parallel knowledge base system. Parallel production systems are also presented since they give insight to the various architectural, optimization, and performance alternatives of parallel rule execution. Finally, following the previous part of the book, we present a parallel object-oriented knowledge base system, named PRACTIC^{KB}, that adapts the rule integration techniques of DEVICE onto a parallel object-oriented database system.

5 PARALLEL DATABASE SYSTEMS

In this chapter we overview some of the issues of parallel database systems, including object-oriented systems. This discussion is vital for understanding several issues related to concurrent processing of data in parallel systems. The material presented here will help understanding the parallel execution of rules in parallel knowledge base systems, in the next chapter.

In this chapter we mainly focus on parallel execution of queries for different query types, algorithms and architectures supporting such queries, and, finally, data distribution techniques that help executing queries in parallel. The chapter concludes with a presentation of the few parallel object-oriented database systems that have emerged so far.

Introduction

Modern data-intensive database applications strive for enhanced performance. In the past decades several special database machines [83] have appeared in order to speed up database operations by using special purpose hardware. However, their high cost and the moderate price/performance ratio did not allow them to enter the database market successfully. The major problem of database systems is the I/O bottleneck [25], i.e. the orders of magnitude difference between memory and disk access time.

In order to reduce the I/O time, *parallel database systems* [51, 141] that combine the technology of multiprocessing with database systems have emerged. Parallel database systems divide the data into multiple processors and disks of a multiprocessor system and, thus, reduce the I/O time by executing queries in parallel among the multiple processors and disks.

An orthogonal direction for the search of performance improvement for time-lined database applications is main-memory database systems [62]. The integration of the above two research directions have been studied in the context of the PRISMA/DB project [8].

Many parallel database systems have appeared, both as research prototypes, such as BUBBA [24], GAMMA [50], VOLCANO [70], and XPRS [135], and as commercial products, such as TANDEM NonStopSQL [74] and TERADATA DBC/1012 [44], to capture the demand for speed in database processing.

A common place for all the above systems is that they are all relational database systems. This is not a coincidence, though, since relational databases are based on a simple, set-oriented data model which is easy to distribute among multiple sites. Furthermore, the data manipulation language of relational databases, SQL, is a high-level declarative language with few processing constructs that is easy to optimize and execute in parallel.

However, new applications of database technology, such as design and concurrent engineering applications, integration of heterogeneous, independent databases, applications involving multimedia data, etc., require advanced data representation features. Object-Oriented Databases (OODBs) [9, 71] are an intersection of object-oriented ideas and conventional databases that reflect the growing need of both designers and users for a representation tool that is semantically richer than that provided by relational databases.

In OODBs, the relationships between data (objects) are explicitly stored as pointers from object to object. In contrast, relational databases need costly join operations to uncover the relationship between different entities stored at different relational tables. Therefore, OODBs outperform relational databases when operations on single objects and their related ones are performed because the relationship pointers are directly followed, whereas a relational database would perform a join.

However, the performance of OODBs for complex queries that involve several relationships between several different types of objects is limited due to their sequential implementation. Recently in order to overcome the above limitations *parallel OODB systems* have been proposed [14, 55, 94, 137, 141], following the research for parallel relational databases.

Although several of the solutions adapted for parallel relational databases can be applied also to parallel OODBs, there are some distinct issues in the management of OODBs that cannot be tackled using the relational database techniques. These include complex objects, querying, object-oriented database programming languages and their processing, and transaction processing [141].

In this chapter we briefly overview some of the issues related to parallel database systems, in general, and parallel OODB systems, in specific. We concentrate the discussion on issues such as architectures for parallel database systems, data partitioning techniques, parallel query processing algorithms, and parallel object-oriented data models.

Parallel Query Execution

The main objective of introducing parallelism in database systems is to increase the performance of the system. Ideally, when a parallel database system runs on a multiprocessor system with N processors then its performance must be N-times better than the monoprocessor equivalent system. Or, to put it in other words, the multiprocessor system should be able to run N-times harder applications than a monoprocessor system with the same performance.

However, applications are not so easy to parallelize. The execution of operations among the N processors is not always independent from each other; therefore, one processor should wait for another to finish in order to get the results or read the data that the other processor just modified. Such interdependencies, along with processor initialization and communication costs, deviate real systems from the ideal linear behavior. In order to measure the "goodness" of a parallel database systems *speed-up* and *scale-up* are used.

Speed-up S is the fraction of the performance of the monoprocessor (or sequential) system in a given application to the equivalent performance of the multiprocessor system, both working on exactly the same application.

$$S(N) = \frac{R_{seq}(P)}{R_{par}(N,P)}$$

In the above equation, R is the performance of a system in whatever units is counted in and P symbolizes the problem size. The closer the speed-up is to the linear behavior N (or at least αN), the better the parallel system.

Scale-up L is the fraction of the performance of the monoprocessor system to the equivalent performance of the multiprocessor system. However, the multiprocessor system is working on an N-times harder problem.

$$L(N) = \frac{R_{seq}(P)}{R_{par}(N, NP)}$$

The closer the scale-up is to 1, the better the parallel system.

Database Query Types

Database queries can be classified into two broad categories: Decision Support queries and On-Line Transaction Processing (OLTP) queries. *Decision support queries* are complex, retrieval queries that are used in order to "discover" useful information from large amounts of data. For instance, a simple decision support query, in SQL, is the following:

```
SELECT NAME,POSITION
FROM EMP
WHERE SALARY>500000 AND AGE<30
```

The main features of decision support queries are that they are not so often issued, they may involve more than one relations (through joins), they take a lot of time and system resources to complete, and they may return a lot of tuples as answers.

On the other hand, *OLTP* queries are simple, retrieval and modification queries that are used to find and modify some tuple(s) in the database that match certain criteria. An OLTP query could be the following, for example:

```
UPDATE EMP
SET SAL = SAL*1.15
WHERE NAME = 'Nick'
```

Contrasted to decision support queries, OLTP queries are very often, especially in dynamically changing databases, such as airline reservations and banks, they complete in a short time "touching" only a few records of the database, and they usually do not return answers, apart from acknowledgments or error messages.

The differences between these types of queries are so large that no database system can run both of them simultaneously in a completely optimized way. Usually, there are separate systems for these two different database uses or these queries run on the same system but on different times of the day. This separation has been proved viable, since the target data of these query types are different. More specifically, OLTP queries involve highly changing, every day data, whereas decision support queries involve more stable data, which are probably aggregates (e.g. sums, averages, etc.) of the everyday data.

In the following subsections we describe features and issues concerning both OLTP and decision support systems since both are useful for understanding issues related to parallel knowledge base systems. OLTP systems give an insight to locking, a concurrency mechanism that has also been used to maintain correctness in the parallel execution of rules in a database environment. Decision support systems, on the other hand, mostly involve the efficient detection of complex associations among data which can be actually used to match rule conditions.

Parallelism in OLTP systems

The performance objectives of these two types of database systems are quite different. OLTP requires high *data availability* and *transaction bandwidth*. When multiple users are accessing the same database concurrently, some kind of concurrency control must be maintained by the system. This means that when one user is accessing some tuples for reading or writing them, then another user cannot write those tuples at the same time. He/she must wait until the first user *commits* the transaction. On the other hand, many users can simultaneously read the same piece of data. Concurrency control is usually maintained by *locking* the data to be used.

A *locking protocol* must guarantee that all transactions are *atomic* and *serializable*. A transaction is atomic if it consists of many data modifications and all or none of those modifications are performed on the database. When multiple transactions are executed concurrently each one of them must be serializable, i.e. the results of each transaction must be the same as if all transactions were executed sequentially, one after another.

The *two-phase locking protocol* guarantees the above properties by using two types of locks: read or shared locks and write or exclusive locks. Before a transaction reads data it must acquire a read lock on them. If other transactions have already read locks on the same data, then there is no problem with concurrency. On the other hand, write locks are acquired exclusively by the transactions that want to write data. If one transaction has a write lock then another transaction cannot acquire either a read or write lock on the same piece of data. This would violate the consistency of the data and the serializability of the involved transactions.

All locks are released after all needed locks have been acquired first. Usually this happens at the end of transaction. Since users have to wait sometimes for the data to be unlocked it means that data may be unavailable and the transaction completion time may delay, compared to a single-user system. An efficient concurrency control strategy aims at reducing the time the data is unavailable by intelligently granting and releasing locks. When the average delay time is reduced then more transactions will complete per time unit. The performance of OLTP systems usually is counted on transactions per time unit.

Deadlock may arise in databases when two or more transactions try to obtain locks that are mutually granted to each other. For example, the first transaction requires a read lock on item A while the latter is write locked by the second transaction. At the same time, the second transaction requires a read lock on item B that is write locked by the first transaction. Common solutions to the deadlock problem are the requesting and granting of locks in some predetermined lexicographic order or the use of special run-time deadlock detection mechanisms that abort one of the deadlocked transactions, non-deterministically, releasing all its locks.

The benefits from parallelizing an OTLP system are focused on the concurrent execution of multiple transactions. When transactions involve data that are stored at different processors/disks then these transactions can be executed in parallel increasing the transaction bandwidth. This is called *inter-transaction parallelism*.

However, the problem of data availability remains when two transactions request the same data simultaneously. In order to increase data availability some piece of oftenly accessed data are replicated across the disks of the parallel system. In this way, many users can simultaneously access the same piece of data. *Data replication* introduces the problem of *data consistency*. When multiple copies of the same piece of data exist then there must exist a mechanism to update all these copies efficiently when one of the copies (called *primary copy*) is modified. Furthermore, two copies cannot be updated differently at the same time. Finally, an invalidating scheme must inform transactions that have read a piece of data that it has changed.

A problem caused by the distribution of data in multiple processors/disks is that certain data are not easily locatable and transactions lock more resources than needed. This reduces data availability. For example, in the OLTP query example at the beginning of this section, the search for an employee named 'Nick' must be performed at all the processors that hold different parts (also called *partitions*) of the relation EMP.

If most queries involve selections of employees based on their name, then a "clever" distribution of tuples of employees based on their name would probably make the location of 'Nick' to certain known processors easy. This would release the rest of the processors from the load of executing a useless query and increase data availability. This and other partitioning strategies will be better presented in the next section.

Some other forms of parallelism that are mostly important for decision support queries are analyzed in the following subsection.

Parallelism in Decision Support Systems

Decision support queries may or may not be issued in a multi-user environment. If all queries in the system are retrievals then concurrency control is not needed. Multiple queries submitted to the system can be answered concurrently or one after the other. However, the performance metric of transaction bandwidth is not so important here. The performance of the system is measured by *query response time*. The distribution of data across multiple sites and the parallel execution of queries aims at reducing the response time.

Intra-transaction or *intra-query parallelism* is achieved when a query is executed in parallel. Intra-query parallelism can take two forms.

Some relational operators, such as selection and join, can be applied in parallel among the different data partitions that are scattered to the multiple processors and disks of the system. This is called *data* or *partitioned parallelism* and it depends on the data distribution. For example, in the decision support query example at the beginning of this section, the search for highly paid, young employees can be performed in parallel among all the processors that hold different partitions of the relation EMP. The results of these queries are then combined into one set and given back to the user.

Clever distribution of data is also important in parallel decision support systems, however, the objective of data distribution is not high data availability but the homogeneity of distribution. To be more specific, in the previous example, if all employees that meet the selection criteria are placed into one processor, then query execution becomes sequential for this processor while the rest of them will sit idle. The query would execute faster if the desired employees were equally distributed to all processors. In this way the processing power of all processors would be exploited. The effect of data concentration in one or few processors is called *data skew*.

If a large query contains nested subqueries, then nested queries are answered first, their answers are forwarded to the outer query, and another round of query distribution is started until the large query is completely answered. Each individual subquery can be executed using partitioned parallelism; therefore, completely independent queries are executed in parallel. This is called *inter-operator parallelism* and it depends on the query.

A bottleneck problem occurs when the results of the nested queries must be combined and fed to the outer query. In order to avoid this bottleneck, the outer query does not have to wait until the nested queries are executed to completion. Instead when some of the results of the nested queries are available these can be fed to the outer query which processes them and possibly forwards them to another query and so on and so forth. This is called *pipelined parallelism* and it depends also on the query.

Parallel join execution. The most useful and expensive relational operator in decision support system is join. Joins combine tuples of two or more relations based on the common value of some attribute(s). For example, the following query prints the names and the departments of employees that earn more than a certain amount. Since EMP and DEPT are different relations, a join is required to combine the names of employees and the departments they work in.

```
SELECT EMP.NAME, DEPT.NAME
FROM EMP, DEPT
WHERE EMP.SALARY>500000 AND EMP.DEPTNO=DEPT.DEPTNO
```

A naive approach to joining two relations would require the retrieval and examination of the product of the number of tuples of the two relations. Therefore, it is easily understood that the parallelization of joins is crucial for the performance of decision support systems.

Several efficient algorithms have been developed for performing joins in sequential and parallel database systems, such as the nested-loop method [54], the sort-merge method [124, 148], and the hash join method [52, 96]. The last of them is the most successful one, unless data skew is present.

Hash join algorithms distribute the two relations into *hash buckets* based on the value of the join attribute. Each bucket of both relations with the same value is stored on the same processor. The join between the two relations is restricted now to the join of the bucket pairs that can be done in parallel. The problem of data skew in hash join appears when one bucket pair is considerably more expensive to join than the rest. This is usually tackled by dynamically distributing the bucket load to processors [96].

When more than one joins exist in a query then there are multiple alternative *query execution plans* for the *multi-join queries*. The correct selection of a query execution plan can increase the amount of parallelism within the query. For example, for a 4-way join A-B-C-D, the order can be left-to-right ((A-B)-C)-D or balanced (A-B)-(C-D). The latter can execute the two inner joins in parallel and then execute a join on the results of the first two. The former seems to require more steps because it is sequential, however, a pipeline among the three steps of joins can increase the performance. These alternatives that depend on the actual database system should also be considered by the *query optimizer*.

Parallel Database System Architectures

There are two prominent architectures for parallel database systems: *shared-everything* and *shared-nothing*. Between these two extremes lie shared-disk systems, which did not attract major commercial or research interest and we will not further analyze them.

Shared-Everything Architecture

With this architecture all the processors of the system share in a symmetrical way all the main-memory modules and disks of the system (Figure 7).

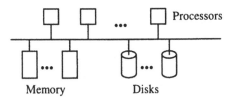

Figure 7. Shared-everything architecture

The advantages of this architecture are the following:

- Intra-transaction parallelism is very easy to implement because each new transaction is a new process that is allocated to another processor.

- Load balancing is easy to achieve, when more processes than processors exist. Each new process can be allocated to the least occupied processor. Furthermore, process migration is relatively easy since only one piece of code with few main-memory data has to be moved.

- Inter-transaction parallelism is relatively easy for read-only queries. Certain costly relational operators, such as sort and join, can be parallelized using classical parallel algorithms from the parallel programming research area.

- Finally, inter-processor communication is achieved in a fast way using the main-memory.

The main problem of shared-everything architectures is their limited scalability. When the number of processors increases (e.g. more than 32) then the bus that connects the processors with the disks and memory is contented due to concurrent processor-to-memory access requests. The result is that adding more processors to the system does not improve or even worse degrades its performance [51].

Most commercial database systems, such as ORACLE, DB2, SYBASE, have been ported to shared-everything architectures, like Unix workstations and mainframes. However, commercial systems exploit only inter-transaction parallelism which is very easily achievable. There are few research prototypes, such as XPRS [135], that exploit intra-transaction parallelism as well.

Shared-Nothing Architecture

In the shared-nothing architecture, each processor has its own private memory and disk (Figure 8). Therefore, data stored in the disk of one processor are not directly accessible to another. Processors communicate in a message-passing fashion.

This architecture offers a solution to the major database problem: I/O bottleneck. Each relation is distributed across every processor disk and even a simple select/project query can benefit since the retrieval of tuples is done in parallel by the processors from their own disks. All types of parallelism that have been mentioned in the previous section can be efficiently exploited.

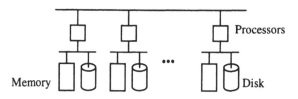

Figure 8. Shared-nothing architecture

The shared-nothing architecture offers great scalability (to thousands of processors) since data exchanged between processors are relatively few and the inter-connection hardware cannot be easily contented. Of course, good scalability also means that the performance can be increased by simply adding new processors to the system. In the next section we will show that eventually there is an upper bound to the scalability of these systems, as well.

The main problem of shared-nothing architectures is load balancing. When certain processor/disk modules are more oftenly accessed than others, these can become performance bottlenecks. This problem has been identified in the previous section as data skew for parallel decision support systems. Furthermore, it can cause low data availability in multi-user OLTP systems. Potential solutions to load balancing are data replication, that has been analyzed in the previous section, and non-uniform data distribution, that will be analyzed in the next.

There are many parallel database systems based on a shared-nothing architecture both as commercial products, such as Tandem NonStopSQL [74] and Teradata DBC/1012 [44], and as research prototypes, such as Bubba [24], Gamma [50], Volcano [70]. All of them support both inter- and intra-transaction parallelism.

Hybrid Architecture

Comparing the above two architectures, it can be concluded that shared-everything systems are best for load balancing while their scalability is limited, whereas shared-nothing systems have the exactly opposite properties. Therefore, a hybrid architecture that offers both good load balancing and scalability seems more appropriate for future systems [21].

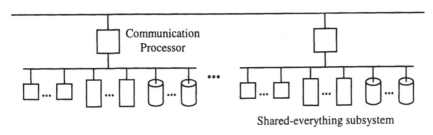

Shared-everything subsystem

Figure 9. Hybrid architecture

Such an architecture would be comprised of shared-nothing modules. Each module would be a shared-everything subsystem, i.e. it would have processors that share memories and disks. Query execution at both the global level would be executed in parallel (due to the shared-nothing architecture) and the local level (due to the shared-everything architecture).

Most importantly, the load at each local level can be balanced due to the shared-everything architecture. Finally, the system would be scaleable because new shared-everything modules can be added easily (global shared-nothing architecture). The extensibility, of course, of the local shared-everything systems would be limited but also not so intensively needed.

Data Partitioning

The purpose of data partitioning is to distribute data into multiple processors/disks so that I/O and query execution on different pieces of data may be performed in parallel. There are two types of partitioning a database: horizontal and vertical partitioning.

Horizontal partitioning is the distribution of different tuples of a relation into different disks. Each partition has exactly the same schema (i.e. number of attributes) as the original relation. Horizontal partitioning allows all kinds of parallelism mentioned in previous sections, because different queries or even the same query can be executed in parallel among the different partitions.

Vertical partitioning is the split of a relation into a set of relations-partitions. Each partition has a schema that is a subset of the schema of the original relation. Each tuple of the original relation is now split into several tuples of each partition. In order to obtain the original tuple one has to join one tuple from each relation. Vertical partitioning allows more I/O parallelism since each attribute of a tuple is retrieved in parallel. Furthermore, data availability is also increased since queries access and lock only the relevant attributes.

The main disadvantage of vertical partitioning is the expensive reconstruction of the original relation through a series of joins among the vertical partitions. Furthermore, its I/O parallelism is rather fine grained and not likely to affect the performance of large decision support queries. On the other hand, its main advantage is the increased concurrency since transactions access only very relevant portions of data. Therefore, it is most suited for OLTP systems.

In the following we will only consider horizontal partitioning since it can offer a much more scaleable solution to parallelism, depending only on the number of available processors. On the other hand, vertical partitioning can be scaled only up to the number of relation attributes

Horizontal Partitioning Strategies

There are three horizontal data partitioning strategies: round-robin, hash, and range partitioning.

Round-robin partitioning. This is the simplest partitioning strategy. Each subsequent tuple of a relation is distributed to a different disk of the system in a circular fashion. Round-robin is ideal for general purpose queries because it distributes the tuples homogeneously regardless of their attribute values. Therefore, queries are likely to access all partitions distributing equally the workload.

Hash partitioning. According to this strategy, tuples are placed on partitions by applying a hashing function on an attribute. The function specifies the placement of the tuple on a particular disk. When a query requests some tuples with a certain value for the hashing attribute, then this query can be forwarded only to one or few disks, based on the hashing function. In this way the overhead of starting a query to multiple disks is avoided. Furthermore, the rest of the disks can be used by another query, increasing the inter-transaction parallelism.

Range partitioning. This strategy places tuples with close attribute values to the same disk. For example, employees whose age is between 25 and 34 are placed on the same disk. Range partitioning is extremely application dependent. It is good for range queries compared to hash partitioning which is better for single hit queries. However, it occupies more space because an index of ranges to disks must be maintained.

In order to avoid data skew where all accesses are made to one partition, range partitioning may create non-homogeneous partitions for a certain attribute, based on the access frequency of each partition rather than its size (number of tuples) [43]. However, this variable partitioning is more suited for small, OLTP queries, rather than large decision support queries, where the access frequency for all partitions are likely to be the same because decision support queries do not usually have a pre-determined access pattern so that customized indices can be built.

Finally, a remark that is valid all partitioning strategies is that when the criteria used for data placement change to the extent that load balancing degrades significantly, *dynamic re-organization* of partitions is needed. An important issue is on-line re-organization without stopping the normal system execution. Furthermore, re-organization should be transparent to all transactions. This can only happen if partitions affect only the physical and not the logical database schema and transactions are unaware of the underlying partitioning scheme.

Scalability Limitations

The number and size of partitions affects the execution time of a query since the finer the partition size, the faster query execution ends. However, there is a limit beyond which the reduction in the size of the partition is not justified because the query startup cost exceeds the query execution cost. The behavior of data parallel query execution has been analyzed in [147] for PRISMA/DB, a parallel, main-memory database system. However, the analysis is valid for disk-based database systems as well, provided that certain parameters are changed.

Uniform partitioning. Considering the shared-nothing architecture of Figure 10, the master processor of the system receives a query and based on the partitioning strategy it distributes it to the appropriate partitions (slave processors). The

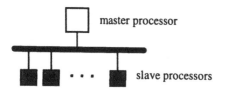

Figure 10. Master-slave architecture   Figure 11. Parallel query execution

distribution includes query initialization and acknowledgment costs, along with inter-processor communication overhead. The initialization is done sequentially by the master; therefore, query execution is not started on each processor at exactly the same time.

Assuming that all partitions are equal, the time behavior of query execution is depicted in Figure 11. It is proved, in [147], that the scalability of such a system is limited, i.e. one cannot add processors to decrease the query response time ad infinitum.

The speed-up of parallel execution is:

$$S = \frac{\alpha + cN}{\alpha n + cN/n}$$

where α is the initialization time of each slave processor, c is the processing time per tuple in respect to a specific relational operator, N is the total number of tuples of the relation, and n is the number of slave processors that the relation is distributed into. The speed-up increases monotonically until a certain number of processors:

$$n_o = \sqrt{cN/\alpha}$$

Further increase in the number of processors would incur a degrade in the speed-up. It is obvious that for a given relation size the only way to increase the scalability of the system is to increase c which is unacceptable because it increases the query response time or to decrease α, i.e. optimize the implementation of the database system. The maximum speed-up is:

$$S_o = n_o/2$$

i.e. half the linear (ideal) speed-up. The main reason for such a deviation from the ideal behavior is that slave processors do not start nor end together; therefore, most of them remain idle before the beginning and after the end of query processing.

Finally, the system's scale-up is decreased as the number of processors increases [13]. This means that adding more processors does not help the system at solving harder problems, at least not as much as ideally expected. This ability is also monotonically decreasing.

$$L = \frac{\alpha + cN}{\alpha n + cN}$$

Non-uniform partitioning. A non-uniform partitioning strategy that avoids the idleness of processors after the end of query processing has been proposed by Bassiliades and Vlahavas, in [13]. The result is that processors are utilized more and the system can be scaled to about 40% more processors than the uniform partitioning.

The time behavior of query execution under the non-uniform partitioning is shown in Figure 12. Each partition after the first one is smaller than the previous one in order to end at the same time since it starts later due to the unavoidable sequential initialization overhead. The speed-up of such a system is proved to be:

Figure 12. Non-uniform partitioning

$$S = \frac{\alpha + cN}{\frac{1}{2}\alpha(n+1) + c\,N/n}$$

The system is scaleable up-to $\sqrt{2}$ or 41.4% more processors than the uniform partitioning. The maximum achievable speed-up is also 41.4% better.

$$n_o = \sqrt{2\,cN/\alpha}$$

Finally, the non-uniform partitioning scales-up ideally, i.e. $L=1$, until the n_o processors. Beyond that point a system re-organization is needed. The uniform partitioning, instead, can operate beyond n_o with sub-optimal performance.

Parallel Object-Oriented Database Systems

The parallelization of OODBs has not yet received much attention mainly because the main research effort in the early years focused on the improvement of OODB structural capabilities and performance through conventional optimizations. Furthermore, many of the basic techniques of parallel relational databases are directly applicable to parallel OODBs.

Research has been mainly focused on parallel persistent object-oriented programming, rather than databases with their demand for efficient query support. Many papers have been written about distributed OODBs but these techniques are not really applicable for a true parallel OODB.

There are very few papers in the literature [15, 53, 55, 94, 137] and even fewer systems [14, 23] that consider the parallelization of OODB management in a multiprocessor environment.

Objects are independent, autonomous computational entities that encapsulate their state information (data) and their behavior (programs). The nature of objects implies a very simple parallel execution model for object-oriented systems. Each object may be executed concurrently in a separate process in a multiprocessor environment. Concurrent processes can cooperate via message sending on a message-passing multiprocessor machine or via shared variables in a shared-memory architecture.

Several concurrent and/or parallel object-oriented programming languages have appeared, such as ACTORS [5], POOL [7], MENTAT [73], etc. In all these languages instance objects are the basic concurrent units of computation.

In a realistic application, however, the number of concurrent objects are more than the available processors and some objects may have to share a processor. Since no memory is shared in a message-passing environment, the above approach is efficient only when the number of objects is small, otherwise the system will clutter from two factors:

- time overhead caused by the switching of context when an object receives a message;

- memory space overflow caused by copying methods [28] from a class to its instances.

In most object-oriented applications, objects are *coarse-grained* computational units. However, things are different in OODBs where instance objects represent the actual data. Therefore, instance objects are fine-grained entities which cannot be possibly mapped on separate processors. Furthermore, in OODBs there is a greater interest in efficient query processing, rather than efficient execution of general purpose computations.

The AGM database system [23] does not consider the above drawbacks and is based on an instance-object level of concurrency. AGM is based on an entity-relationship model where the relationship between instances is explicitly stored. During query execution the links between interrelated objects are retrieved and followed by propagating tokens in an asynchronous manner. The asynchronous execution improves parallelism because centralized control of concurrent queries is avoided. However, for large OODBs with many users the propagation of tokens at the object level will create significant overhead cost.

This navigational style of query processing in OODBs contains a substantial, inherent amount of sequential execution as it is argued by Kim, in [94]. Pre-computed relationships (joins) between objects create chains of interrelated objects; therefore, a query can only be evaluated by accessing the first object in the chain and sequentially following the links from object to object. There is not much amount of parallel execution in such a query processing style.

Kim identifies and analyzes three types of parallelism in OODB queries [94]. *Path parallelism* exploits the parallel execution of different navigational paths of a query graph. *Node parallelism* is the parallel processing of the nodes of a query graph in respect to simple (local) predicates. Finally, *class-hierarchy parallelism* is the parallel execution of the same query in the different classes of a class-hierarchy. According to the analysis of Kim, only class-hierarchy parallelism can offer significant improvement in query response time.

The multiprocessor architecture of Kim allocates one class to each processor of a shared-nothing machine where the communication cost between any two processors is the same [94]. Furthermore, it is assumed that this cost is small compared to the query processing cost and is ignored in the analysis. Since the number of classes in an OODB is fixed the system cannot be scaled to large numbers of processors in order to improve its performance.

The architecture that is used in the OSAM system [137] further distributes a class into vertical partitions. Each class partition may or may not be stored on a different processor. The evaluation of queries is done in two steps. First the objects selected by the query are marked and then the attributes requested by the query are retrieved.

In addition to the types of parallelism mentioned above, vertical partitions introduce the possibility for parallel retrieval and predicate testing of different attributes of the same object. However, this requires the extra overhead of intersecting the results obtained from two different vertical partitions of the same class. Furthermore, the number of attributes for a class is fixed; therefore, there is no scalability possibilities in this architecture. Finally, as mentioned in the *Data Partitioning* section, vertically partitioned systems are more suited for OLTP systems, rather than decision support systems.

The most useful feature of a parallel system is its scalability. If the system is seamlessly scaleable then its performance can be improved by adding more processors until a certain "saturation" limit. The scalability can only be achieved if the database can be distributed into many components. Furthermore, these components should be easily degradable in order to allow more processors to be added and the components to be divided into smaller components so that the load is equally distributed to all processors.

The PRACTIC parallel OODB system [14, 15] is based on a two-level hierarchical architecture in order to achieve high scalability. The first level manages the schema classes while the second one manages the class extensions. Therefore, in addition to the types of parallelism that are mentioned above, PRACTIC also supports *intra-class parallelism* which allows the parallelization of query processing inside the class. The instance objects of each class are partitioned into a number of processors of the second level that "belong" to exactly one processor of the first level.

Hierarchical query processing proves to be quite faster for class-hierarchy queries. This is mainly due to the fact that the initialization of the second level processors is not done sequentially for the entire array but chunks of the second level processors are initialized in parallel by the first level processors. Furthermore, the object distribution can be adjusted so that the second level processors can be "shared" by adjacent classes. This sharing improves the utilization of the system resources. More details on hierarchical processing are presented in chapter 7.

In addition, PRACTIC is one of the few systems that are based on a concurrent object-oriented data model. The model (also analyzed in chapter 7) is driven by the usefulness and functionality of each object type and assigns resources only to the objects that are vital for speeding up query execution. The following assumptions about an OODB are used:

- the number of instance objects is large because they represent data;
- the number of classes may vary but is considerably smaller than the number of instances;
- there are only few meta-classes in a typical OODB system.

An important distributed OODB that uses many features of parallel OODBs is SHORE [32]. SHORE is a client-server distributed OODB which consists of a network of servers. Each server is a workstation that can also host a client application. The local server of each client is responsible for finding, locking, and fetching the appropriate pages that contain an object requested by the client. The object can either reside locally or at a remote SHORE server.

An important issue addressed by SHORE is how data placement at the servers affects performance [143] where it is concluded that it is better to decluster an aggregated complex object into many servers rather than cluster it in one server. However, this result is hardly surprising since declustering a complex object is similar to vertical partitioning.

The parallel processing of the declustered complex objects is performed through the ParSet construct [55]. ParSets are collections of objects on which operations can be performed in parallel. It is a quite generic operation that is used by the database programmer to parallelize an application. SHORE does not have an ad-hoc query language but provides some basic database programming constructs to programming languages, such as C++.

As database programming languages are computationally complete and far more expressive than ad-hoc query languages, their optimization is an extremely difficult task. In OODBs, the mostly used programming constructs are loops over sets of objects which also contain nested loops that navigate through the objects' complex attributes. The optimization and parallelization of these loops has been studied in [53] where several pointer-based algorithms are presented.

6 PARALLEL KNOWLEDGE BASE SYSTEMS

In this chapter, we discuss the various theoretical and implementation issues and approaches to parallel knowledge base systems. The main problems concerning parallel execution of rules are: how to speed-up the matching of rule conditions by distrubuting them in a multiprocessor machine, and how to execute rules in parallel in such a way that the sequential semantics of rule programs are preserved. The discussion includes parallel production systems, parallel deductive, and parallel active databases.

Introduction

Rule processing in expert systems and databases has been slow mainly due to the sequential execution of rules. However, the bottlenecks for the two different systems are quite different. Real-world expert system applications tend to have thousands of rules while the size of their initial and intermediate data (facts) is considerably smaller. On the other hand, rule database systems usually deal with millions of data stored at secondary storage devices while the rule base size does not usually exceeds hundreds of rules.

As modern advanced applications require more intelligence and concern vast amounts of data these two system types tend to merge into expert database systems. However, as it was discussed in the previous chapter, parallel processing is required in order to increase the performance of such a system.

The parallel execution of rules imposes several more difficulties than the mere integration of rules in database systems that was discussed in the first part of the book. The most important of the problems are: a) the architecture of the system, b) the distribution of rules and data, c) the interference problems that the concurrent rule execution generates, and d) the problem of controlling the execution of rules in parallel.

In the following we discuss the above problems along with the solutions proposed by various researchers and implemented in various systems. We begin the discussion with parallel production systems both for main-memory and database expert systems. Production rules are very important since their parallelization issues are a superset of the issues of the other rule types, and, historically, production systems were the first that posed those problems and offered some solutions. Then, we present specific techniques for evaluating deductive rules in parallel deductive databases. Finally, the more recent trend of parallel execution of ECA rules in active database systems is discussed.

Parallel (Database) Production Systems

There are two main bottlenecks in the execution of production rules. The first is the matching of production rule conditions which has been reported to consume as much as 90% of the computation time spent on production rule execution [60]. The other is the execution of a single rule at each production cycle.

Parallel Condition Matching

The speed-up of condition matching against the working memory and/or the database was initially attempted using various techniques, such as the discrimination network approaches that have been presented in chapter 2. Additional speed-up can only be achieved by parallelizing rule matching in a multiprocessor environment.

Under a naive parallelization scheme, the RETE network can be mapped onto a very fine-grained message-passing multiprocessor architecture by assigning each node of the network on a processor. The tokens exchanged between nodes are messages sent between processors. This simple scheme can cause two problems:

- If a change in a working memory element (WME) causes the same node of the RETE network to be activated multiple times, then this node will be come a bottleneck since the processor that hosts this node can only process the multiple activations sequentially.

- Each processor hosts one node of the RETE network. However, only a small subset of the nodes are activated at any given time. Therefore, the utilization of the multiprocessor machine is very low. The utilization can be improved by allocating several nodes to a single processor. This, however, could reduce parallelism when multiple nodes, assigned to the same processor, are activated simultaneously.

The last problem above can be ameliorated by using clever node-to-processor allocation techniques. Such an approach has been followed by Gaudiot and Sohn [65] where a special-purpose data-flow multiprocessor machine has been used to match the RETE network in parallel. One-input nodes (or α-memories) of the same condition element share the same processor along with the left or the right memory of a successive two-input node (or β-memory). Repeated condition elements are replicated to processors in order to reduce inter-processor communication.

Despite the clever allocation of the RETE network nodes to processors, the first of the above problems cannot be tackled using such as very fine-grained scheme. To resolve it, the nodes that are likely to bottleneck the execution should be identified and given more resources in order to cope with the increased computation.

During the match phase, the most of the time is spent in processing two-input nodes, which perform a join between the left-input and the right-input memory and vice-versa. A more realistic (and coarser-grained) approach to parallelizing rule matching is to allocate a two-input node to multiple processors. More specifically, the tokens that reside at the memories of two-input nodes are stored in different processors. When a token arrives at the left memory then the join with the tokens of the right memory is performed in parallel among the processors that the right memory tokens are stored into.

In order not to occupy all the processors of the left/right memory the tokens are hashed to processors using the join attribute. In this way the processor(s) that is (are) more likely to host matching tokens is (are) identified and the rest of the processors are not involved in the join procedure. This procedure resembles the hash-join algorithm for parallel join that has been presented in the previous chapter.

Acharya et al. presented, in [4], two alternative architectures that employ the above technique. In the first, fine-grained architecture, there are different processors for each left and right hash buckets. Furthermore, there is a small number of processors dedicated to one-input nodes and for conflict resolution. A second, coarser-grained architecture merges one-input nodes into the processors that perform joins for two-input nodes. In addition, the conflict set is performed by a single control processor. Finally, the equivalent left and right hash buckets for two-input nodes are in the same processor.

The latter architecture is, more or less, used by Richeldi and Tan, in [120], to perform parallel matching of production rules for large databases. The difference is that Richeldi and Tan use the TREAT instead of the RETE algorithm and that α-memories are hosted at different processors than the ones that perform the hash-join.

An even more coarse-grained approach is used by Stolfo, in [134], where production rules are distributed among a number of processors. WME changes are distributed to all processors and matching is performed in parallel among the processors. Each processor places the matched rule instantiations in its local conflict set and a separate processor merges them and performs global conflict resolution. Several variations of the above scheme have been implemented on the DADO family of multiprocessors.

Gupta [75] uses a hashing strategy in order to avoid the duplication of all WME tokens to all the processors. Specifically, the constant tests of rule conditions are used to distribute the WMEs to the processors that contain relevant production rules.

Finally, PARULEL [133] uses two approaches based on the distribution of WMEs into subsets that reside at different processors. The *blocking approach* distributes the WMEs into blocks which are not necessarily disjoint subsets. Each block is assigned to a single processor along with the whole rule set. Again each processor has a local conflict set which is used for global conflict resolution when all processors complete their local production cycles. However, this approach can only be used heuristically since processors do not communicate with each other during the rule matching and some combinations of WMEs may be missed.

The *copy-and-constrain* [132] or *data-reduction* [150] approach is more complete since it cannot miss any rule instantiations. WMEs are again distributed to multiple processors. Rules are copied to multiple processors but each rule is constrained (by introducing constraint tests in the condition) to match a subset of the WMEs matched by the original rule. Special care is taken to ensure that the entire set of copies computes the same conflict set of rule instantiations as the original rule.

Processors do not communicate during rule matching since the rule re-writing technique guarantees that each constrained rule needs only locally present WMEs. However, after the rule actions are executed the WME modifications are communicated to the appropriate processor.

Several other approaches [10, 29, 90, 106] exist in the literature for matching production rules in parallel. However, we believe that the approaches we presented above are the most representative ones.

In the next chapter we present in detail production rule matching and execution on the PRACTIC^{KB} parallel knowledge base system which is actually a parallelization of a RETE-like network.

Multiple Rule Execution

The most important bottleneck of production rule systems is the selection and execution of a single rule instantiation from the conflict set at each production cycle. There are many cases where multiple rule instantiations can be safely executed at the same cycle. This has two benefits:

• The number of cycles is reduced. Therefore, the overhead associated with the management and control of each cycle is reduced. This mainly benefits sequential production systems.

• The multiple rule instantiations can be executed in parallel. This reduces the execution time of each cycle. This, of course, benefits only parallel production systems.

A special case when multiple rule instantiations can be executed in the same cycle is when these are instantiations of the same rule. For example, consider the following production rule:

```
IF a(X) & b(X,a) THEN delete(a(X))
```

If there are multiple WMEs of classes a and b that match the above production rule then all the corresponding rule instantiations can be selected for execution in the same cycle. This has been actually used in production database systems, such as RDL1 [100], ARIEL [78], DEVICE [18], etc., where set-oriented semantics are more preferable than tuple-oriented semantics of the OPS5-like production systems.

However, it must be noted that the semantics of rule execution regarding conflict resolution is slightly changed due to the set-oriented nature of rule execution. Specifically, a case might arise where a rule that waits in the conflict set for a long time is promoted and executed due to a recent single update [78]. This difference is inherent in the set-oriented approach.

In the most general case, every rule instantiation can be executed in parallel. However, there are two problems associated with this unrestricted parallelism: *serializability* and *control*.

When all rule instantiations are executed in parallel, then the result of a set of production rules can be different from the result produced by any equivalent sequential production system with any rule execution order. Serializability restricts parallelism in order to guarantee that the results of parallel rule execution are serializable, i.e. equivalent to at least one sequential rule execution.

Rule interference. Rules are not serializable when they interfere. *Interference* of rules appears in two cases: *read-write* and *write-write interference*.

Read-write interference. Read-write interference appears when one rule modifies in its action a WME that is read by the condition of another rule.

```
R₁:   IF  a(X)  THEN  delete(b(X))
R₂:   IF  b(X)  THEN  add(c(X))
```

Rule R_1 disables rule R_2 above by deleting a WME that is positively referenced by rule R_2. Therefore, if both rules are present in the conflict set, then the result of the above program depends on the order of execution in a sequential production system.

For example, if WMEs $a(1), b(1)$ exist in the WM then the rule instantiations $\{R_1, a(1)\}$ and $\{R_2, b(1)\}$ will both be in the conflict set. If R_1 is executed first then WME $b(1)$ is deleted and the instantiation of rule R_2 is removed from the conflict set and never executed. On the other hand, if R_2 is executed first, then $c(1)$ is added to the WM. Then R_1 is also executed and $b(1)$ is removed from the WM.

This simple form of read-write interference does not cause a problem in parallel rule execution. If the above rules were executed in parallel, then the first one would remove $b(1)$ from the WM without affecting the second rule which would add $c(1)$ in the WM. The result of the concurrent execution of the two rules is identical to the second sequential execution we described above.

The problem with read-write interference is caused by cyclic rule references. For example, in the following triple of rules each one disables the other when executed sequentially. The result of the execution depends on the order the rules are executed.

```
R₁:   IF  a(X)  THEN  delete(b(X))
R₃:   IF  b(X)  THEN  delete(c(X))
R₄:   IF  c(X)  THEN  delete(a(X))
```

If, e.g., all $a(1), b(1)$, and $c(1)$ WMEs are present, then the execution order R_1-R_4 (R_3 is disabled by R_1) would result in $c(1)$ being left in WM; the order R_3-R_1 (R_4 is disabled by R_3) would leave $a(1)$ in the WM; and, finally, the order R_4-R_3 (R_1 is disabled by R_4) would leave $b(1)$. If, however, all rules are executed at the same time then none of the WMEs is left in the WM. This result is not serializable because it cannot be produced by any sequential execution.

The examples given above show read-write interference when the action of a rule deletes a WME that is positively referenced by the condition of another rule. However, the same interference exist when the action of a rule inserts a WME that is negatively referenced by the condition of another rule.

```
R₅:  IF a(X) THEN insert(c(X))
R₆:  IF b(X) & ¬c(X) THEN add(d(X))
```

If $a(1), b(1)$ exist in the WM, and R_5 is executed first, it disables R_6 because it inserts $c(1)$ while R_6's condition states that $c(1)$ (in conjunction with the existence of $b(1)$) should not exist.

Write-write interference. Write-write interference appears when two rules modify in their actions the same WME in a contradictory manner.

```
R₇:  IF a(X) THEN delete(c(X))
R₂:  IF b(X) THEN add(c(X))
```

Consider, in the above example, that WMEs $a(1), b(1), c(1)$ are present. If, rule R_7 is executed first then $c(1)$ is deleted. Then R_2 is executed and $c(1)$ is re-inserted. In case $c(1)$ was not originally present in the WM then the action of R_7 either would be ignored or an error message would appear. If execution follows the opposite order, then $c(1)$ is added by R_2, if it does not exist, or just ignored otherwise. Then, R_7 deletes $c(1)$ anyway.

The concurrent execution of both rules would produce either of the above results since the two contradictory actions cannot really be executed concurrently but in a non-deterministic order. The real problem with parallel execution and write-write interference appears when rules perform multiple actions.

```
R₈ :  IF a(X) THEN delete(c(X)) & delete(d(X))
R₉:  IF b(X) THEN add(c(X)) & add(d(X))
```

Working as above, the sequential execution would leave either both $c(1), d(1)$ in the WM or none. The non-deterministic concurrent execution of the above rules could produce any of the following results: $\{c(1), d(1)\}, \{\}, \{c(1)\}, \{d(1)\}$. Some of them could not have been produced by any sequential execution.

The serializability problems we described above have been mainly tackled using two ways: *dependency graph analysis* and *locking*.

Dependency graph analysis. The serializability problems can be avoided if a production rule dependency graph is built and analyzed during the compilation of rules. The dependency graph reveals potential rule interferences which are then used at run-time to prohibit the concurrent execution of interfering rules.

The rule dependency graph is a graph whose nodes are either rules or WMEs. When a WME is positively referenced in the condition of a rule, then there is an arc from the WME node to the rule node, augmented with the plus '+' sign. A negatively referenced WME would have the negative '-' sign instead. When a rule action inserts a WME then there is a positive arc from the rule node to the WME node. A negative arc indicates that the rule action deletes the WME instead. For example, the dependency graph between example rules R_1, R_2 is shown in Figure 13.

Figure 13. A sample dependency graph

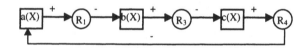

Figure 14. A cyclic read-write interference

Figure 15. A simple write-write interference

When there is a read-write interference between two rules then a WME node receives a negative arc and emanates a positive one, or vice-versa (Figure 13). A cyclic read-write interference is identified by a cycle in the graph where arcs are labeled by alternating positive and negative signs (Figure 14). When the graph contains cycles then the problem of mutual disabling we analyzed above can appear when all rules are executed concurrently. In order to guarantee serializability it suffices to prohibit the concurrent execution of one of the rules in the cycle with the rest of the rules.

A write-write interference in the graph is detected when a WME node receives two arcs with different signs (Figure 15). However, the example in Figure 15 does not cause a real concurrency problem as we explained earlier but we use it here for simplicity. The problem with write-write interference is caused with at least two such WME nodes. Again the solution is to serialize the execution of such interfering rules.

The reader should notice that the dependency graph analysis reveals only possible rule interferences and not actual ones. This happens because the values of the variables of the WMEs are not known until run-time. For example, in Figure 14, if WMEs $a(1)$, $b(2)$, and $c(1)$ are present in the WM, at run-time then the cycle of the dependency graph is broken and there does not exist a serializability problem at all.

If the compile-time analysis is based only on the possible interference of rules, not taking into account the possibly different rule instantiations, then the serializable rule execution plans are very restrictive. This means that they execute rules sequentially far too often than it is actually required. The result of this is that the parallelism potential is severely restricted. This kind of analysis was followed by Ishida and Stolfo [88] who pioneered the work on serializability using dependency graph analysis. Also the RUBIC system [104] follows this rule-level dependency analysis and parallel execution.

An improvement to the rule-level analysis is the instance-level analysis of the dependency graph [87, 108, 122]. The instance-level analysis takes into account the format of the variables and constant tests in condition elements and WME modifications of rules. As a result certain rule interferences that limit the amount of parallelism in parallel rule execution are avoided.

For example, in the following pair of rules, a rule-level analysis would indicate that rules R_{10}, R_{11} have a read-write interference whereas a deeper analysis at the rule-instance level reveals that the WME that is deleted by rule R_{10} could never disable rule R_{11}; therefore, these two rules can be safely executed concurrently.

```
R₁₀: IF a(X) THEN delete(b(X,1))
R₁₁: IF b(X,2) THEN add(c(X))
```

The above analysis can still be done in compile-time. However, there are cases when one cannot be certain at compile-time if interference will occur at run-time. For example, in the following pair of rules, rule R_{12} deletes WME $c(X,Y)$ that is positively referenced by rule R_{13}. However, the values for variables X, Y cannot be determined at compile-time. Variables X, Y in rule R_{13} do not only depend on WME $c(X,Y)$ but are also bounded by the WME $d(Y,X)$. Therefore, sometimes these two rules may interfere and sometimes they may not.

```
R₁₂: IF a(X,Y) & b(Y) THEN delete(c(X,Y))
R₁₃: IF d(Y,X) & c(X,Y) THEN add(w(X,Y))
```

In order to cater for such cases a run-time analysis is needed as well. At run-time the instantiations of these two rules are known. Therefore, if variables X, Y are not the same for the two rules, then these two rules can be executed concurrently. Run-time tests are "costly", however, and it is appropriate to use them only when there are many possible rule interferences and the speed-up gained by executing them in parallel outperforms the overhead of run-time checking.

Finally, there are cases, such as rules R_1, R_2 in the beginning of this subsection, where the variables that appear in the WMEs are not bounded by other WMEs. In such cases, it is most safe to execute these rules in some sequential order, unless extremely "expensive" run-time tests are performed. Of course, this does not mean that rule instantiations are definitely going to interfere but that there is a great possibility for this.

Similar analysis can be performed for write-write interferences but we omit it for brevity.

Numerous systems have appeared in the literature that execute multiple production rules in parallel. Above we have presented some that are based on guaranteeing serializability using either rule-level or instance-level rule interference analysis.

Special mention should be made for the CREL system [98] which uses the TREAT algorithm [103]. CREL employees an instance-level static rule analysis to partition the rule set into independent rule clusters. Each rule cluster is executed asynchronously, in parallel. Clusters communicate via message-passing. Rules within the cluster may execute in parallel, based on run-time analysis. CREL does not perform any other conflict resolution policy, apart from the rule-interference analysis.

An important shortcoming of CREL is that clusters are rarely executed in parallel since the clustering is based on a very simple, syntactical analysis of rules. In each cluster rules that perform the same task are placed in much the same way as the Means-Ends-Analysis strategy of OPS5 [59]. Different tasks are mostly executed sequentially by changing the value of a WME that plays the role of the *flag*.

The PARULEL system [133] gets one step further by eliminating traditional conflict resolution strategies altogether. Instead, conflict resolution is definable in terms of meta-rules that redact the conflict set. Therefore, the resolution semantics are very flexibly enforced by the programmer instead of the system. After meta-rules remove redundant rules from the conflict set the remaining rule instances are executed in parallel, asynchronously. No serialization is enforced.

An important issue regarding PARULEL is how the system is going to determine when no more rules enter the conflict set in order to start evaluating the meta-rules. It seems that some synchronization is needed at that point. However, in the PARADISER environment [49] these issues have been resolved by mapping the semantics of PARULEL onto Datalog** [149] and executing the latter using an incremental algorithm that caters for asynchronous updates (see next section). Meta-rules are just a second level rule processing task that matches rule instantiations in the conflict set instead of the working memory.

Locking. Another way to ensure serializability of parallel rule execution is locking of WMEs, a technique that has been used both for databases [118, 130] and main-memory production systems [105]. Locking has been used for concurrency control in database systems (see previous chapter) to ensure serializability and atomicity of transactions. If parallel executing production rules are considered as separate transactions then they can coexecute asynchronously, provided that the locking protocol guarantees serializability.

The approach of DIPS [117, 118] follows the usual two-phase locking protocol. Each rule-transaction obtains a read lock for specific tuples it positively depends on, i.e. for tuples identified by a positive condition element. For negative condition elements the rule must obtain a read lock for the entire relation since the insertion of any tuple may invalidate the negative condition.

If the rule condition is confirmed, i.e. the query of the condition returns a non-null set, then the action must be executed. Since rule actions involve data modifications write locks must be acquired before the action is executed for the tuples that a rule deletes or modifies. These tuples have been read locked by the same rule before; therefore, the lock manager should convert the read lock into a write lock, unless other rules hold read locks on the same tuples. In the latter case the rule must wait until the read locks are released.

Finally, if a rule inserts tuples on a relation it must obtain a write lock on the entire relation. This is needed in case the relation appears in a negative condition element of another rule.

To see why this locking scheme enforces serializability consider the simple case of rule interference of Figure 13. If, for example, rule R_1 acquires its write lock on tuples b(X) (where X stands for specific value or values) before rule R_2 acquires a read lock on the same tuples, then rule R_1 will be executed only. If, on the other hand, rule R_2 acquires the read lock first, then rule R_1 will be delayed until rule R_2 runs into completion and releases the locks. Then rule R_1 will be able to execute. Both of the above behaviors are serializable.

A deadlock problem can occur in cyclic interference cases. In the example of Figure 14, all three rules can obtain read locks on the WMEs of their conditions but none of them can obtain a write lock to execute its action. Therefore, all three rules will be frozen waiting for the rest to release their read locks which normally would never happen. The usual solutions for deadlock situations in databases can be used (see previous chapter).

A variation of this technique has been used by Srivastava et al. [130] where read locks on condition elements and write locks on action modifications are allowed to be granted at the same time. Of course, these conflicts are recorded and used at each rule's commit time to enforce rule serializability and data consistency. When a rule that holds a read lock commits before a rule that holds a write lock on the same data item, then the result is serializable. On the other hand, when the rule with the write lock commits first, then the rule with the read lock must be forced to abort because the modification of a data item referenced in its condition might invalidate the rule. Alternatively the rule's condition can be re-evaluated to check for invalidation.

Finally, a similar locking scheme adapted to the main-memory UMP-OPS5 production system has been presented in [105]. A notable difference with Raschid et al. [118] is that write locks for the action are acquired at the same time with the read locks for the condition, i.e. much before action execution is about to begin. This, of course, limits concurrency but prevents deadlock. A rule that cannot acquire all of its read and write locks at the beginning cannot start executing.

Another important difference of the locking scheme of UMP-OPS5 is that it does not lock entire relations to enforce serializability in case of negated condition elements for the sake of performance. Instead, they use a list of items to be added by rule actions and they check the negative condition elements against this list, even before locks are acquired. This technique allows more concurrency among rules because entire relations are not locked but has the drawback that the list of added items would potentially become a bottleneck. Furthermore, the distribution and maintenance of this list can prove cumbersome.

The PRACTIC^{KB} (see next chapter) uses a locking scheme similar to Raschid et al. [118]. However, all the schemes presented in this section consider parallel execution of rules which are distributed to multiple processors while data is centralized. This makes the locking and execution algorithms easier. The PRACTIC^{KB} system instead distributes data among the processors in a shared-nothing multiprocessor machine. Furthermore, in PRACTIC^{KB} there is a new rule priority locking scheme for controlling rule execution.

In general, the benefits of using a locking scheme instead of performing rule interference analysis is that locking always works in the same way, while rule analysis does not always provide accurate results. Locking always provides the maximum amount of concurrency. On the other hand, locking is performed entirely at run-time, adding overhead to the rule execution time. Finally, as a conclusion it can be said that locking is preferable when there is no heavy interference between rules.

Control. Serializability seems to be a loose criterion of correctness. *Convergence* [99] is a more strict criterion that requires the parallel rule execution to not only produce the same result with some serial execution order but with a controlled sequence of execution. If rules are guaranteed to be serializable and produce the correct (or preferred) solution then they are executed in parallel. Otherwise they are executed sequentially.

The above criterion is used in RUBIC [104] along with the notion of contexts. Each *context* is a cluster of rules among which the convergence criterion is enforced. Contexts can be activated either sequentially or in parallel. Contexts is a similar notion with the rule clusters in CREL [98]. However, their main difference is that in CREL clusters are derived syntactically while in RUBIC they are explicitly defined by the programmer.

Constructs similar to contexts (named tasks) have been used by Neiman [105] to control parallel rule execution. However, Neiman uses serializability through locking to enforce correctness. Furthermore, the quality of solutions is determined by using static rule priorities. Rules of different priorities are incrementally placed into separate queues and high priority rules are executed first. However, this solution is not complete since high priority rules might appear in the conflict set after the low priority rules have already committed their execution. Such cases are handled by choosing different control strategies for each task, including sequential programming constructs where necessary.

In PRACTIC^{KB}, a rule priority scheme for control is used. However, it must be noticed that rule priorities are used by the rule processor to synchronize the rule execution order. Priorities can be derived from higher level constructs, such as the ones presented in this section or even traditional conflict resolution techniques.

Synchronous vs. asynchronous execution. In a multiprocessor environment each processor executes the basic Match-Select-Act loop of production systems. If all processors are synchronized at the end of the matching phase in order to perform conflict resolution, then parallel rule execution is synchronous. The drawback of synchronous execution is obvious; the slowest processor determines the total execution time while the rest of the processors remain idle.

A much better, in terms of performance, solution is that each processor proceeds at each own pace. This severely reduces the chances for conflict resolution in terms of control while serializability can be addressed either by locking or by rule interference analysis. One of the solutions that have been adopted is to reject conflict resolution and provide control constructs, such as rule clusters, which can be treated differently than the default case.

The PRACTIC^{KB} system, presented in the next chapter, supports a novel rule priority locking scheme that enforces correct conflict resolution in a distributed memory environment where rules are executed asynchronously. Rule priorities can be used to emulate several high-level conflict resolution criteria.

Another solution is to provide some truth maintenance technique in order to control the inferencing process. Early conclusions that are later proven false can be retracted and their effects be completely undone. Such a truth maintenance technique has been used in PARADISER for deductive rules [149] and has also been used for mapping the semantics of production rules [49].

Shared vs. distributed memory architecture. Shared-memory multiprocessor machines tend to be easier to program and load-balance. However, they are more expensive and they cannot be scaled-up to many processors due to the contention of the shared memory. Shared-memory architectures can be used both for synchronous and asynchronous parallel rule execution. Rules are distributed to processors while WMEs reside in the shared memory. Locking is also advantageous in shared-memory machines because data are kept in one place.

On the other hand, distributed memory machines are more difficult to program and load-balance because the sharing of data can only be done through message passing between the processors which is a costly operation. The greatest benefit of distributed memory architectures is that they can be safely scaled-up to many processors provided that algorithms can be distributed effectively.

There can be different distribution schemes for such machines. Either rules or data can be distributed to the processors. If one distributes rules only, then data has to be replicated across every processor which wastes a lot of memory. Furthermore, different copies of the same data exist which can cause consistency problems [123]. Synchronous execution in such a framework gives an opportunity at the end of each cycle to distribute the changes of the data to each processor. Asynchronous execution calls for temporal database inconsistencies that can be resolved through complicated acknowledgment protocols [123].

Another alternative is to distribute data to processors and replicate rules which do not require consistency maintenance. Each piece of data resides in a unique processor; therefore, no data inconsistencies occur. An important issue is to be able to locate the processor of a certain piece of data easily. This is usually achieved through hashing, as in the data-reduction method [150].

Another important issue is to be able to avoid extensive communication among the processors because communication is costly. Much of the communication overhead is due to the matching of rules. When the condition of one rule needs to match data that reside in different processors then these data must be remotely sent to the processor that hosts the rule. In order to avoid this, clever allocation of rules and data needs to be made. Again, the data-reduction method [150] addresses this problem by altering the condition of each rule copy (that resides on a different processor) in such a way so that they need to access only locally stored data. Only the results of rule evaluation need to be communicated across the processors. More on data reduction will be described in detail in the next section.

The PRACTIC^{KB} system (chapter 7) is built on top of a parallel OODB system on a distributed memory architecture. Rules are distributed according to the data distribution and the class hierarchy. Inter-processor communication for rule matching is used provided that in modern hardware communication is much faster than it used to be.

Parallel Deductive Database Systems

The problem of executing deductive rules in parallel seems to have more straightforward solutions than production rules. The bottom-up evaluation of deductive rules is quite similar to the forward chaining evaluation of production rules, as it has been explained and demonstrated in part I of the book. However, the "action" part of deductive rules is actually an insertion (or deletion) of a single data item. Therefore, the problems with write-write interference we described in the previous section do not hold. Furthermore, the absence of arbitrary modifications makes the analysis of rule interference easier. Finally, the execution of deductive rules is not heuristically done through conflict resolution strategies but the execution order is strictly defined in terms of stratification.

Actually, only one general parallel execution scheme for deductive rules has appeared in the literature from individual researchers [61, 150]. We will refer to this scheme as *data reduction*, as it has been used for Datalog** [150]. Data reduction, as we have already explained, is a technique that distributes rules to processors in such a way so that the rules do not have to communicate with other processors in order to match their conditions.

Decomposing of data and rules is achieved by partitioning data to processors according to a measurable criterion, such as a hash function, and then adding this criterion to the condition of the local rule copy. In this way the local rule copy will be "forced" to match only locally stored data. For example, consider the transitive closure of the arc relation.

```
path(X,Y)  :- arc(X,Y).
path(X,Y)  :- path(X,Z), arc(Z,Y).
```

The tuples of the arc relation are partitioned to k processors via a hashing function $h(X)=i$ on the first attribute, where i is the processor that the arc(X,Y) tuple resides. Therefore, the non-recursive rule above can be transformed to a set of rules in the following form:

```
path(X,Y)  :- arc(X,Y), h(X)=i.
```

Each of the above rules is stored on a different i processor and matches the tuples of the arc relation that reside exclusively on the same processor. The hashing function of the recursive rule is a little more complicated and can be different from the hashing function of the first rule.

```
path(X,Y)  :- path(X,Z), arc(Z,Y), h'(X,Z)=i.
```

The hashing function h' must be one that does not allow the above rule at processor i to match both path and arc tuples that reside at nodes different from processor i. For example, a pair of such hashing functions follows, provided that the attributes of path and arc relations are integer numbers or that they can be mapped to integer numbers, one-to-one.

```
h(X)   = (X+1) mod k
h'(X,Z) = (X+Z) mod k
```

However, not all problems are decomposable using data reduction and decomposability of a program is generally undecidable as proved in [150]. Furthermore, decomposability does not preclude communication among the processors. The data derived by a rule at each processor must be further distributed to some remote processors in order to keep the property of local matching consistent.

For example, the recursive rule at processor i must transmit some derived tuples at processor j according to the hashing function for the derived tuples: h'(X,Y) = j. In order to realize why this is so, imagine that a tuple path(5,8) is derived at some point in processor i. This tuple is needed at next iteration because path is a recursive predicate. However, the condition of the rule insists that a rule at processor j matches only tuples of path that fulfill the hashing function h'(X,Z)=j. Therefore, the derived tuple is going to be needed by the processor j for which the equation h'(5,8)=j holds and by no other processor. Thus, the tuple must be transmitted to this processor.

All processors use the same technique for evaluating the restricted rule programs, e.g. semi-naive evaluation. If all processors operate in a synchronous manner then at the end of each cycle all processors transmit their derived tuples to the appropriate processors and the evaluation phase advances to the next cycle. A distributed termination algorithm is needed in order to detect global termination [149]. Synchronous processing has certain performance limitations discussed in the previous section.

An asynchronous version of the above parallel execution scheme has the problem that different processors may evaluate different strata of negated rules. Therefore, it could be possible that a processor receives some derived tuples that invalidate some of the tuples it has already derived. For example, consider the following pair of rules.

```
t(X) :- p(X), ¬s(X).
s(X) :- q(X).
```

Predicate s is at a stratum lower than t because t negatively depends on s. Both the above rules are distributed to all processors using some (may be different) data reduction strategy. If the two rules have different hash functions (for some reason) then when processor i finishes with evaluating s and increases its stratum by evaluating t, another processor j may still be evaluating s. Therefore, if processor j transmits derived s tuples to processor i then some of the derived t tuples at processor i may be illegal according to the tuples received from processor j.

In order to overcome the above inconsistency problem an asynchronous algorithm that incrementally maintains the locally derived tuples has been presented in [149] for the PARADISER system. This algorithm stops at each cycle and before proceeding to the next checks if another processor has send some derived tuples. If these tuples belong to a lower stratum than the stratum of the processor in question, then a nested evaluation phase takes place that calculates the effects of the received tuples for the local and remote databases.

When the nested evaluation phase reaches the current stratum, the evaluation continues normally with the next cycle. If the received tuples belong to the current stratum, then they are just incorporated to the local database and the next cycle begins. Finally, if the tuples belong to higher stratum, then they are just ignored because they cannot affect the local evaluation.

The PRACTIC[KB] system (chapter 7) is also based on stratification for asynchronously evaluating deductive rules in parallel. Strata are used to provide rule priorities and then deductive rules are evaluated in the same way with production rules. The correct global rule execution order is maintained by a distributed rule priority locking mechanism. This mechanism alone suffices to preserve serializability of parallel deductive rule execution without the need to obtain locks on data, as for production rules.

Apart from the data partitioning approaches some data-flow approaches have also appeared in the literature [20, 68, 86]. These approaches base parallelism on the distribution of rules among processors and the pipelining of data produced from one rule to the other according to the rule dependency graph. Global termination is achieved when each of the rules have terminated producing intermediate results and all messages have been forwarded through the communication channels. However, these fine-grained approaches do not utilize the resources when some specific paths in the computation are used while some others remain idle. Furthermore, they involve much communication among the processors while the actual workload of each processor per transmitted tuple is too small.

Transitive Closure Queries

A special type of deductive rules is linear recursive rules, i.e. recursive rules with no negation and a simple recursive call in one of the rules. The rest of the rules are not recursive. This type of rules is also called transitive closure query because it represents the transitive closure of a relation using a simple, recursive relational query. A typical example of a transitive closure query is the path derived relation example we have given before. Due to this most typical example, transitive closure queries are also called *path queries*.

The parallelization of path queries has received considerable attention by the parallel database research community. The various approaches that have been devised are much alike the ones we have described for parallel deductive rules. Specifically, there are both data-flow approaches [31, 119], and data fragmentation approaches [6, 38, 142].

The data-flow approaches assign relational operations to different processors and there is a pipeline among them that processes the tuples of the original and the recursive relations. The principles of the data fragmentation approaches are much the same with the ones we described for parallel deductive rules and we omit their description for brevity. The main objective of the various alternative approaches is how to load balance the parallel hash-join algorithm.

A completely different parallel execution scheme is the disconnection set approach [81] which is based on semantic fragmentation. This approach instead of distributing data using a hash, it divides the graph of arcs (or any other arc-like relation) into loosely connected subgraphs. Each subgraph is assigned to a processor. All processors work in parallel and calculate the paths within their subgraph. Upon completion the partial paths of the different processors must be joined to produce total paths. Performance measurements of this algorithm on the PRISMA machine has shown even super-linear speed-up for certain graphs [82].

This coarse-grained approach, although peculiar, it actually models a real-world problem of finding railway or road connections between two cities in different countries or regions. Each country is a natural fragment (subgraph) of the total connection graph and the problem is divided into a set of sub-problems. Each sub-problem finds the best route across a country. Then, the intra-country routes must be combined across the borders of two countries.

Parallel Active Database Systems

Parallel active databases have not yet received much attention in the literature since active databases is a relatively new research area. Very few papers [34, 84] and only one system, named OSAM*.KBMS/P [136], have appeared so far. A common element in all the above approaches is that they do not introduce new issues but instead they re-use techniques used for parallel production rules, such as rule graphs and locking.

The algorithm proposed by Hsu et al. [84] is concerned with detecting triggered active rules in a distributed environment. Their method algebraically decomposes complex rule conditions into multiple conditions evaluated in distributed database sites. The rule condition is analyzed in order to identify independent parts of the condition that can be evaluated in parallel with minimum communication overhead among the sites. Although condition evaluation is distributed, rule processing is centralized.

The evaluation is based on data-flow execution in a hierarchical master-slave organized computation. The decomposed query is a tree where the leaf nodes calculate their results in parallel (slaves) and forward them to the upper nodes (masters), until the root node of the query is reached. This means that the condition of the rule has been satisfied. Each interior node synchronizes its children nodes.

In Ceri and Widom [34], various locking mechanisms are described for the execution of active rules in parallel and distributed environments under various assumptions about rule interference, priorities, and asynchronous execution at remote sites. Their main locking mechanism is similar to the locking mechanism of Raschid et al. [118] except that they differentiate between transaction locks and rule locks.

Asynchronous rule execution is supported by Ceri and Widom, in [34], by introducing two new locks for the local sub-transactions of a global transaction and for the current state of the triggered rules. These locks guarantee that rule processing at a site does not start before all local sub-transactions have been executed. If the latter is the case then rule processing is rolled back and synchronization is enforced. Finally, entire relations are locked in order to guarantee that: a) the triggering environment of a rule does not change while the rule has been selected but not yet executed, and b) that a higher priority rule is not triggered after a lower priority rule has been selected but not yet executed.

Finally, rule ordering, using priorities among rules of different sites, is achieved by obtaining locks on entire relations whose modification triggers rules of lower priority than the currently executing ones. This locking is done on every site for each currently running rule. The locking schemes of Ceri and Widom [34] are correct but they introduce many new rule locks, complicating lock management. Furthermore, the locking of entire relations at multiple sites may severely restrict the parallelism of rule execution. Their algorithms are easily adaptable to parallel databases with horizontal partitioning.

The system OSAM*.KBMS/P [136] is also based on a two-phase locking protocol for parallel rule execution. The main feature of the system, apart that it is built on top of a parallel OODB system, is the control of rule execution which is based on an explicit partial ordering among the rules instead of implicit priorities or other conflict resolution techniques.

Their active rule language allows the association of an event with a rule graph instead of a single rule. Each rule graph defines a partial ordering among that set of rules. This means that the same set of rules can be re-used in another rule graph that is triggered by another event. Such a fine control on rule execution is proved useful in problems where the same chunks of knowledge are combined in different sequences for different tasks, such as diagnosis problems.

Another special feature of this system is that rule processing is uniformly embedded in a graph-based transaction model that is more flexible than nested transactions or tree transactions. This allows parallelism among no interrelated rules to be governed by the laws of transaction concurrency. Rules that are ordered in the rule graph are executed sequentially.

Asynchronous rule execution is achieved in the implementation on a shared-nothing multiprocessor. They use a master-slave architecture where the master processor distributes sub-transactions of a global transaction (including rule activations) to the slave processors that may induce other sub-transactions that are handled again by the master processor.

The instances of all the classes of the OODB are distributed to all the slaves. The evaluation of the condition of each rule is done in parallel using the asynchronous parallel querying techniques presented in [137]. These algorithms have been described in the previous chapter.

The PRACTIC^{KB} system (chapter 7) uses different parallel execution modes for different types of active rules. Specifically, ECA rules are generally characterized by their immediate or deferred nature. Immediate rules are executed without taking into account a global execution order but only a local one. Deferred rules are executed using a mechanism similar to Ceri and Widom [34]. However, PRACTIC^{KB} enforces correct execution order by a novel rule priority locking mechanism that avoids wide locks on entire relations. Furthermore, immediate and deferred rules triggered by the execution of deferred rules are treated uniformly but their relative execution order is strictly determined by the application semantics of each rule type.

7 A PARALLEL OBJECT-ORIENTED KNOWLEDGE BASE SYSTEM

In this chapter, we present in detail a parallel object-oriented knowledge base system, called PRACTIC^{KB}. PRACTIC^{KB} implements the rule integration techniques of the DEVICE knowledge base system (presented in chapter 4) on top of a parallel object-oriented database system, named PRACTIC [14, 15]. The implementation of DEVICE in PRACTIC involves issues concerning the distribution and parallel execution of complex event detection and rule processing.

In the following, we first present the object-oriented model, multiprocessor architecture, and parallel query execution algorithms of PRACTIC. Then we extend the model and architecture by integrating the DEVICE techniques for multiple rule support.

The Parallel Object-Oriented Data Model

The PRACTIC OODB system is based on the PRACTIC concurrent object model. The word PRACTIC means PaRallel ACTIve Classes. The term *active* should not be confused with active databases that have been described in chapter 2. Here the term *active* means the representation of classes by permanent concurrent processes that exist in memory and always run a background procedure in addition to servicing messages.

Active classes describe and aggregate their instances, and are responsible for the management of their instances. The resulting model is a vertically partitioned system [85] since both abstraction and functionality are encapsulated inside the classes.

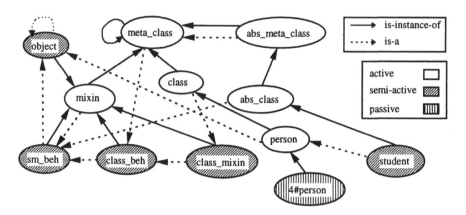

Figure 16. Instance hierarchy of PRACTIC objects

In PRACTIC model, objects are classified according to their ability to have instances (directly or indirectly) and/or to be able to generate new ones. There are three types of objects in PRACTIC (Figure 16): active, semi-active, and passive objects.

Active Objects

Active objects are defined as the objects that: a) have direct instances, and b) can create new instances. They are called active because they are permanent processes in memory. This is vital for being able to respond at any time to messages that request the creation of new instances, the retrieval of old instances, etc. Moreover, active objects do not remain idle when they are not servicing a message but they execute a background procedure to monitor the efficient management of their extensions.

Active objects are: a) all the user-defined classes of an OODB schema except of the abstract classes, and b) some of the meta-classes, described in the following.

PRACTIC supports both pre-defined meta-classes and meta-classes supplied by a model designer to tailor the data model [97, 112]. We have adopted the terminology and instance hierarchy of ADAM [71, 109] which is essentially the same for any type-less, class-based OO system, such as SmallTalk [69] or Loops [131].

The meta-class hierarchy of PRACTIC is quite different from ADAM since the functionality of the three types of objects according to their "activity" must be incorporated into the meta-class hierarchy. According to the PRACTIC meta-class hierarchy (Figure 16) the active meta-classes are all the instances of the special pre-defined meta-class meta_class which is the top of the instance hierarchy, i.e.

every other meta-class is created by sending it a new message. Notice that `meta_class` is included since it is an instance of itself. The meta-class `meta_class` is essential for the model designer to create new meta-classes that extend the functionality of the OODB [97, 112].

Apart from `meta_class` other active meta-classes include:

- Meta-classes which are responsible for defining user-classes. There can be several of these, as classes may have different properties, e.g. support for keys, relationships, versioning, constraints, etc. [11, 112]. Here two generic meta-classes are discussed (Figure 16), `class` and `abs_class`, which are responsible for creating normal and abstract classes, respectively.

- The meta-class `mixin` which is responsible for creating mixin meta-classes (or *mixins* for short). Mixins hold behavior shared by several pre-defined or designer-defined meta-classes, through inheritance [112].

Semi-Active Objects

Semi-active objects are the objects that: a) have indirect instances, and b) cannot create direct instances. Semi-active objects are not permanent processes but their processes are evoked when a message is sent to them. This is justified by the fact that semi-active objects do not have direct instances to manage. Semi-active object processes are "killed" after they service a message. It is the responsibility of their meta-classes, which are active objects, to monitor messages sent to them and to fork their processes.

Semi-active objects are: a) the mixins [112], and b) the abstract classes [131]. The meta-class `object` is also included as a mixin class. We notice here the difference of our approach to ADAM since we consider `object` as an instance of `mixin` and not of `meta_class` [109]. The `object` mixin is the top of the inheritance hierarchy (Figure 16) for both meta-classes and classes. It defines the general properties of all objects, such as deletion and display. Its indirect instances are both instance objects and classes.

Active and semi-active objects are collectively called *non-passive objects*. Only non-passive objects are connectable through the class hierarchy.

Passive Objects

Passive objects are the objects that: a) do not have either direct or indirect instances, and b) cannot create instances. Passive objects are not permanent processes but mere data structures because they are too many and they do not have instances to manage.

It is the responsibility of their classes, which are active objects, to monitor their state and trigger them to react to messages.

Passive objects are only the instances of user-defined active classes, and they are the actual data in OODBs. In a large database, passive objects are usually many, so there is a need for large storage devices, which can be either disks, for disk-based database systems, or main memory chips, for modern main memory database systems [62].

The Abstract Machine

The PRACTIC model is reflected in the hierarchical architecture of the abstract PRACTIC machine (APRAM). APRAM [15] consists of shared-nothing computational nodes capable of communicating directly with each other via messages through a fully connected global communication network (Figure 17). Each node has its own memory and disk.

APRAM consists of two kinds of processing elements (PEs):

- The Active Object Processors (AOPs), and

- The Active Extension Managers (AEMs).

Active Object Processors

The *Active Object Processors* are the processors where the processes that correspond to the active objects run. They consist of a CPU, memory, and links to other AOPs. AOPs are responsible for: a) running the permanent procedure of the active objects, b) accepting messages destined at either the active object they host or at a non-active

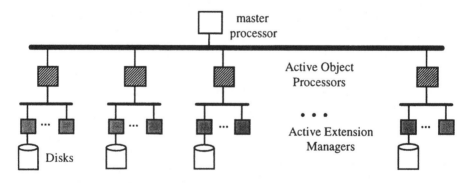

Figure 17. The hierarchical architecture of the abstract PRACTIC machine

instance of the active object, c) evoking the semi-active processes, and d) coordinating query execution for the passive instances on the AEMs.

Semi-active instances of an active object are hosted in the same AOP as their active meta-object to avoid method copy overhead at run-time. Semi-active processes are only evoked on demand and, thus, a) do not occupy much private memory, and b) do not need code from their meta-objects to respond to messages. When a message arrives for a semi-active object, its active meta-object process is suspended and the local scheduler is responsible for evoking semi-active object processes.

Active Extension Managers

The volume of passive instances dictates the need for multiple PEs to manage the extension of active classes efficiently. The *Active Extension Managers* are responsible for processing the passive extension of an active class. AEMs are exclusively devoted to one active class and consequently they are attached to the corresponding AOP. They can directly communicate only to the AOP and to each other, through a local communication network and not to the rest AOPs and AEMs.

AEMs assist active objects by sharing the load of method execution for passive instances. The latter are distributed among the AEMs. This introduces the possibility for intra-class parallelism since the number of passive objects that can be concurrently processed depends on the number of AEMs attached to an AOP. Since I/O has been identified as a major bottle-neck in parallel database systems [51], passive objects are partitioned to multiple disks. However, assuming that AEMs have large enough main memory and the appropriate architectural support [62], the same abstract architecture can be used for a main-memory database system [15].

The existence of multiple AEMs provides a natural declustering for the objects of a class [15]. Declustering criteria can be any one of the popular data partitioning strategies of parallel relational database systems [51], although a hashed partitioning on the OID seems best suited for a general-purpose OODB system. A novel non-uniform declustering strategy has also been proposed to increase the scalability and the performance at the class level [13].

Concurrency of object accesses is controlled by a local lock manager at each AEM. The lock manager is a separate process that is responsible for accepting object lock requests about objects either from remote AOPs or locally. When the lock requests can be granted, then the requesting processor can execute the corresponding query.

Parallel Query Processing

Classes, which are equivalent to relations in relational databases, are the most interesting active objects because they usually have lots of passive instances that are oftenly queried. Meta-classes, on the other hand, neither have many instances nor are frequently queried. In the following, the terms class and active object will be used inter-changeably.

Queries in DBMSs are expressed via ad-hoc query languages which are declarative and expressive but they are not computationally complete. Object-oriented programming languages (OOPLs), on the other hand, can easily support queries expressed using primitive language constructs but they are less declarative. However, query languages are computationally simpler than OOPLs and they can be easily optimized, so that the user does not have to provide optimum access plans.

Ad-hoc queries can be expressed inside the framework of an OOPL by formulating the query in a query language and then translating it into the base OO data language. The query language of PRACTIC is very similar to the rule language of DEVICE that was presented in chapter 4. Specifically, the query is expressed as a rule condition followed by a rule action. The condition is then translated into a set of OODB primitives and runs in parallel against the database. The action is a set of updates to be performed on the selected objects. The action is distributed to the processors of the parallel database system but does not run until the rule condition evaluation is terminated.

```
IF P@person(name:N,age>50)
THEN write(N), nl
```

The above query is translated into the following fragment of the OO data language of ADAM [71], which is Prolog extended with object method invocations via message sending. The translation is done after the query has been optimized using the techniques presented in chapter 4. The symbol ⇒ denotes message sending. On the left of ⇒ is the method selector and on the right is the message recipient.

```
get(P)⇒person, get_age(A)⇒P, A>50, get_name(N)⇒P,
write(N), nl
```

In the following we describe the various types of parallelism during query evaluation, i.e. inter- and intra-class parallelism. The latter can be further sub-divided to inter- and intra-object parallelism. The description is based on simple selection queries as the above one. More complex queries that join objects of different classes are treated similarly to parallel matching of rule conditions. These techniques are presented later, in the section *Integration of DEVICE*.

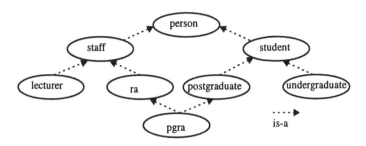

Figure 18. A sample database schema

Inter-Class Parallelism

The classification hierarchy of classes implies a form of OR-parallelism during query execution. According to the translated typical query of the previous section and the schema of Figure 18, the class person has both direct and indirect sub-classes; therefore, the message sent to class person applies to all its sub-classes as well because a sub-class recognizes all the methods of its super-class.

When a class receives a message it re-distributes it to all its direct sub-classes. At the same time it services the message internally by finding all the applicable instances and executing the corresponding method on them. The sub-classes that receive the re-distributed message behave similarly, i.e. they re-distribute the message to their sub-classes, and so on so forth, until a class with no sub-classes is reached.

The results are directly returned to the requesting object, and details about which class produced them are hidden. The complete result is the union of the partial results from each class. Message service proceeds in parallel at each active class involved. Therefore, class-hierarchy implies OR-parallel operational semantics for the inter-class parallel scheme.

When a class terminates the local message servicing process the following alternatives are possible:

- If the class has sub-classes, it just waits for all of them to finish as well.

- If the class has no sub-classes and it is not the target class, it sends an "end-of-message-servicing" (eom) message to its super-class (-es).

- If the class has no sub-classes and it is the target class, it sends an eom message to the sender of the original message.

When a class receives eom messages from all its sub-classes two things happen:

- If the class is the target of the original message, it sends an eom message to the sender of the original message.

- If the class is a sub-class (direct or indirect) of the target class, it sends an eom message to its super-class (-es).

Intra-Class Parallelism

The details of query and method execution inside a class are hidden from the rest of the system as a result of object encapsulation. The system can only "see" the response time of a class to a message. Each class may employ different techniques for parallelizing local query processing to minimize query evaluation time. In the following, we identify two such parallelization techniques that are orthogonal to each other, namely inter- and intra-object parallelism.

Inter-object parallelism. Intra-class parallelism can be achieved, if the activation of passive instances of an active class is done in parallel. In this way, the processing of objects becomes concurrent. This kind of parallelism is equivalent to the data-parallelism of parallel relational database systems and is named inter-object parallelism.

In order to achieve such an internal parallelization an active class needs:

- Multiple active processes devoted to the processing of parts of its extension, and

- Scheduling and coordination among these processes.

Both of the above prerequisites are satisfied within the abstract PRACTIC machine. More specifically, the multiple cooperating processes for the parallel execution of queries on passive instances are mapped onto the AOPs while the coordinator process runs on the AEM.

Object model for AEMs. The distribution of a class into multiple AEMs is not a mere implementation trick but it can be easily fit into the object-oriented data model. Specifically, if each active class is partitioned into a number of direct subclasses (*partition classes*) and each subclass's extension is a non-overlapping subset of the extension of the original active class, then each AEM can host one of the partitions. This kind of partitioning is called *horizontal partitioning*.

The original active class has no longer direct instances and is actually an abstract class itself that aggregates the extensions of its subclasses. However, this abstract class is treated differently from the real abstract classes (semi-active objects) and is assigned resources of the multiprocessor system.

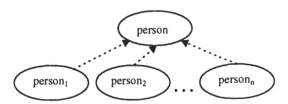

Figure 19. Horizontal partitioning of a class

In Figure 19, class person is partitioned into a number of direct sub-classes. The results to querying the original class person is equivalent to the union of the results to the queries that are distributed to the partition classes in much the same way with inter-class parallelism.

It must be noticed that the partition classes do not have a direct relationship with the partitions of the subclass or the super-class of the active class. This means that querying, for example, $person_1$ will return only the direct instances of this class and not instances of partitions of class student, etc. However, the querying of partition classes is not supposed to be done directly by the user but only indirectly through the active class. In addition, the "isolation" of partition classes fits nicely into the architecture of PRACTIC since AEMs (the processors of partition classes) do not communicate directly either.

Intra-object parallelism. The method inheritance scheme implies parallel execution among the inherited pieces of method code. In order to execute a method on the selected objects the corresponding method body is required. There are three alternative scenarios for the retrieval of method bodies:

- Methods can be totally defined at the current class descriptor, so no inheritance occurs;

- Methods can be totally absent locally, so they must be inherited from a super-class;

- Methods can be specialized versions of definitions in super-classes, so some parts can be found locally and some others must be inherited.

After method bodies are inherited method execution proceeds in parallel at each class. Although the operational semantics of methods are sequential [7], method execution can be pipelined through the tasks of object selection and the execution of inherited method bodies. Methods are still executed sequentially for each object but each process, that is responsible for the execution of a different inherited part of the method, executes on the context of a different object.

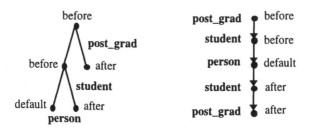

Figure 20. Pipelined method execution

The notion of stream-parallelism between the inherited method bodies can be easily demonstrated using an example (Figure 20). An attribute age is defined at class person along with generic methods for accessing and updating the value of that attribute. If the method concerning the update of age is specialized at a sub-class of person, e.g. student, then the following outline is used [131]:

```
execute code before the default method
delegate message to super-class (default behavior)
execute code after the default method
```

The three stages of method execution are independent but serializable, i.e. the order of execution is always *before-default-after*. This is the most general case. Special cases emerging when any of the three stages is missing are treated in a different manner. For example, if *default* part is missing, then *before-after* parts are concatenated and override the default method. If *before-after* parts are missing then the default method is just inherited explicitly. If all three parts are missing, then the default method is implicitly inherited.

The three-stage method execution holds for every sub-class of person; therefore, a nested graph of independent pieces of code exists. This graph can be represented as an unbalanced binary tree (Figure 20 - left). The root of the tree is the *before* part of method definition at the target class. The left sub-tree represents the default method invocation and can be a tree itself, while the right sub-tree consists always of a single terminal node, the *after* part. Pre-order traversal of the tree provides the correct linearized method execution order (Figure 20 - right).

The linearized order allows the pipelining of the processes on the different nodes. Each node executes a part of the method in the context of a different object at the same time. When a process is complete with an object it forwards it to the next process and receives another object from the previous one. Communication between processes is asynchronous because the processing time of each may differ. This is achieved through the use of queues of objects to be processed.

A full pipelined execution between different method parts can only be achieved if there are enough free processing elements. If there are not, then some of the method parts can be concatenated and executed sequentially on one node. The criterion for this concatenation is the balancing of the computational load among the nodes. Since the computational complexity of each method part may vary, the speed-up that pipeline can offer is bounded by the slowest process in the pipeline. Therefore, concatenating two much faster processes in one does not affect the performance.

Comparison. A simulation of both types of intra-class parallelism, in [14], reveals that inter-object parallelism is slightly faster than intra-object parallelism. Furthermore, pipeline offers only limited speed-up while the data parallelism is bounded only the number of objects and the physical characteristics of the database system [147]. Finally, pipelining occupies much of the system's communication bandwidth since it requires the transferring of objects among nodes.

On the other hand, data-parallelism may suffer from *data skew* when some particular nodes have much more selectable objects for method execution than the rest. Data skew can be avoided by the proper selection of the data partitioning strategy.

Currently in PRACTIC, only data parallelism is implemented since it offers more speed-up than pipelining of method execution. Furthermore, its implementation is straight-forward. Finally, the partitioning of a class extension to multiple AEMs can easily fit inside the object data model. In the future, we may explore the possibility for a hybrid intra-class query processing technique in order to combine the benefits of both types of parallelism.

Hierarchical Query Execution

The combination of inter-class and inter-object parallelism constitutes a two-level hierarchical query execution algorithm that can be ideally executed on APRAM. The outline of the query execution strategy follows. Assume that the system receives a query:

```
IF X@x(<attribute tests>) THEN M ⇒ x
```

where x is the first class of the hierarchy that has k-1 subclasses, and M is an arbitrary method defined on class x and inherited (or overridden) by all its subclasses.

The master-processor (i.e. the AOP of the meta-classes) distributes the query to the AOP of class X and each one of X's subclasses. The master-processor cannot initialize all the AOPs at the same time but each one in turn, sequentially (Figure 21). The AOP receives the query and it starts the method execution processes on each of its AEMs. Again, the AOP cannot initialize all AEMs at once but each one in turn, sequentially.

It is proved, in [15], that the speed-up of such a system cannot be less than a certain lower bound:

$$S \geq \frac{\alpha + cN}{\beta k + \alpha f_{max} n + c \frac{N}{n}}$$

where α is the initialization time of each AOP, β is the initialization time of each AEM, c is average processing time per object in respect to the specific method, N is the total number of objects in all classes, k is the number of AOPs (or classes), and n is the total number of AEMs in every AOP. The quantity f_{max} is the fraction of the workload of the class with the maximum workload to the total workload of all k classes. Therefore, it is less than 1.

$$f_{max} = \frac{c_{max} N_{max}}{cN}$$

The speed-up is maximum for the following number of processors:

$$n_o = \sqrt{1/f_{max}} \sqrt{cN/\alpha}$$

The maximum speed-up has also a lower bound:

$$S_o > \frac{n_o}{1 + \frac{1}{f_{max}}}$$

Figure 21. Hierarchical query execution

It is proved that hierarchical query processing is better than flat processing where all AEMs would be initialized by one master processor, when the following condition holds:

$$\frac{1}{n}\frac{\beta}{\alpha} < \frac{1-f_{max}}{k}$$

Practically, in the usual systems, the following assumptions hold: $\beta \cong \alpha$ and $n >> k$. Therefore, the above condition is mostly true since $1 \leq f_{max} \leq 1/k$.

Overlapping of adjacent class extensions. In order to improve the utilization of the hierarchical system, it has been proposed in [15] that adjacent classes (AOPs) can share their resources (AEMs). This overlapping scheme (Figure 22) allows an AOP to start processing a query locally using the shared resources, provided that its neighboring AOP has not yet initialized the shared AEMs.

The overlapping between classes i and j can only be achieved if the following condition between their workloads holds:

$$\sqrt{c_i N_i / \alpha} \geq \sqrt{c_j N_j / \alpha} + \beta/\alpha + 2$$

The above condition is also a heuristic for finding the optimum class pairs in a system with many classes.

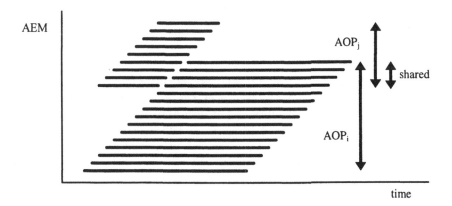

Figure 22. Hierarchical query execution with overlapping

Parallel Rule Evaluation

In this section we present the integration of the DEVICE system, presented in chapter 4, into the PRACTIC OODB model and implementation. There are actually several issues that must be explored, such as integration of event and rule objects into the PRACTIC^{KB} data model, parallel matching of rule conditions, and parallel rule execution.

Integrating Events and Rules into the PRACTIC Model

Events and rules are first class objects in the DEVICE system. Given the data model of PRACTIC where objects are classified into three categories based on the absence or presence of a direct class extension, we can easily see that events and rules do not fit into the established framework of PRACTIC.

Specifically, events and rules are instance objects; therefore, according to the PRACTIC classification they belong to passive objects. The event and rule classes are active objects which should be given exclusive system resources in order to manage their extensions. However, event and rule classes are not usual classes which have to answer to complex queries about their instances frequently. Instead, their instances are pieces of code attached to certain classes and triggered when some operations on these classes (or rather their instances) are attempted.

Therefore, it makes more sense to attach events and rule objects close to the classes they have to guard, much alike methods, instead of storing them to special processors, remotely from the objects they monitor.

A new type of object is introduced into PRACTIC to model events and rules. We call such objects *demon objects*. Demon objects are attached and depend on usual classes; therefore, they are stored in the active classes they monitor. When a demon object is attached to a certain class, it must also be attached to all its subclasses since events and rules are usually inherited by default, except if some exception mechanism is used to confine inheritance [12].

The event and rule classes (and meta-classes) are hosted by the master processor of the APRAM since their management does not require heavy processing. The instances of these classes are distributed to the AOPs (and their corresponding AEMs) of the APRAM. In this way, of course, certain objects are replicated across the system and special maintenance is needed to guarantee their consistency. However, operations on event and rule objects are infrequent and this does not cause an overhead or a consistency problem.

Demon Object Distribution

Simple events are distributed the AOP of the class they monitor and to the AOPs of all their subclasses. For example, consider the event below:

```
event     1#mm_inheritable_ms_event
method    put_age
when      before
class     person
```

This event monitors the instances of class person and, more specifically, it is signaled before the execution of method put_age. The event object is stored in the AOP of class person. If the database consists of the schema of Figure 18, then the above event is also duplicated to the AOPs staff, student, etc. Furthermore, given that a class is partitioned into many AEMs which are actually modeled as subclasses of the active class, the events are also duplicated to all the AEMs of each AOP.

Logical events (see chapter 4) are also hosted wherever the respective simple events are stored. When a logical event has multiple alternative simple input events, then they are duplicated to all such AOPs.

Finally, two different types of two-input events exist to model two different patterns of the rule condition: intra-object and inter-object events. The former models the conjunction of simple and/or logical events that have been signaled for the same object, while the latter models the join of two different objects based on a common attribute. These two patterns have been treated uniformly in sequential DEVICE, despite their obvious differences, in order to keep a uniform event representation. However, in PRACTIC[KB] it is vital to distinguish between these two event types because their distribution policy and run-time behavior are completely different.

Specifically, intra-object events are stored with the class they monitor, much alike simple and logical events. Furthermore, they are duplicated to all the subclasses including their AEMs. On the other hand, inter-object events usually join objects of different classes; therefore, they are distributed to two different classes. However, the distribution is not trivial as the distribution due to inheritance. The two inputs of the inter-object events are from two different classes and the respective input memories are stored at different AOPs. The run-time algorithm for checking if an inter-object event can be signaled requires communication between the AOPs, as we shall describe in the next subsection.

Furthermore, even when an inter-object event joins two different objects of the same class the two inputs can come from two different AEMs of the same AOP because the two different joined objects may reside in different AEMs. Therefore, communication between AEMs inside the same AOP may be required. This is not the case, however, for the intra-object events which join patterns of the same object; therefore, they involve only a single AEM.

Rules are distributed according to the distribution of their triggering events. Therefore, active rules that are triggered by simple events are distributed to all the AOPs that the simple event is replicated. Production and deductive rules are triggered by complex events; therefore, they are distributed to the AOPs that the last event in the discrimination network (usually an inter-object event) is replicated. Furthermore, all rules are replicated to all the AEMs of all the AOPs that they are hosted.

Parallel Rule Matching

The detection of simple, logical, and intra-object events is very trivial. Actually, it is exactly the same as in the case of sequential DEVICE. The event and rule managers are replicated to every AEM of the system. Each AEM, that hosts events, searches in the local event base to find a simple event before or after the execution of a method. If an appropriate event is found, then this is signaled to the local event manager. The event manager then tries to find if the simple event can be propagated through the local discrimination network that includes logical and intra-object events. If rules are triggered by any of these event types, then the local events are signaled to the local rule manager to check if a rule can been fired.

The detection of inter-object events is completely different and it requires distributed algorithms. For simplicity, we will initially present the algorithm using an example of an inter-object event that joins two objects of the same class. Then, we will extend it to capture the general case.

```
IF E@emp(name='Mike',salary:S,salary.manager<S)
THEN delete ⇒ E
```

The rule above involves two intra-object patterns of the same class since the condition is analyzed into the following inter-object pattern:

```
E@emp(name='Mike',salary:S,manager:M) and
M@emp(salary<S)
```

Each AEM of the emp AOP (including the subclasses which can be omitted for simplicity) has a copy of the corresponding inter-object event. Furthermore, the AEMs also have a copy of the left input intra-object event and the right input simple event. When the left (or the right) input is signaled at a certain AEM the incoming token is forwarded and stored at the left input memory of the local inter-object event copy.

Now, the join of the left input token with the tokens stored at the right memory of the event cannot be done only locally because the right memory is distributed and stored across all the AEMs of the emp AOP. This happens because tokens are stored only in the memory of one AEM copy, the one that received the initial simple event that was propagated till the current inter-object event.

The left input token is sent to all the AEMs (including the originating AEM) and the joins are performed in parallel across the AEMs. Notice that, in the above example, the join is on the OID of the manager which is an emp object. Therefore, instead of performing a parallel search among all AOPs the hashing function that distributes objects to AEMs can be used to locate the exact AEM that the matching object resides. When multiple input tokens are processed at the same cycle then the above algorithm turns equivalent to hash join.

The tokens that pass the join predicate (in this example) should be forwarded to the rule manager to indicate that the rule has been fired. The local rule manager at each AEM is responsible to select and execute the rule asynchronously with the rest of the local rule managers. The exact algorithms are presented in the next subsection.

If the two intra-object patterns were of different classes not many things would have changed in the algorithm. For example, in the previous example assume that managers belong to a class mgr instead of being instances of the emp class.

```
IF E@emp(name='Mike',salary:S,manager:M) and
   M@mgr(salary<S)
THEN delete ⇒ E
```

Then the inter-object event would be distributed to AEMs of two AOPs: of class emp and class mgr. The left input and memory would be stored at the AOP of class emp and the right input and memory at the AOP of class mgr. When tokens are signaled at the left input they are stored at the local AEM memory and forwarded to all the AEMs of the right memory. The hashing function for the mgr objects can be used. However, such information about mgr class (and the AOP) is supposed to be hidden away (encapsulation) from the rest of the system. Therefore, the tokens are forwarded to the AOP of class mgr and the AOP is responsible for finding the best way to perform the join, either by using a hashing function or by distributing the query to all the AEMs.

The tokens that pass through the join filtering must be forwarded to the local rule managers that reside at each mgr AEM. Exactly the same procedure would be followed if the right input was signaled. This time the local rule managers of the emp AOP would detect the matching of the rule.

To complicate things further, consider that mgr class is a subclass of emp class. Then, the left input and memory of the inter-object event are distributed to AEMs of both the emp and mgr AOPs (and all possible intermediate classes in the hierarchy). The left input can be signaled either at an emp or mgr AEM, depending on the class of the object that received the original message. The signaled token is stored and propagated to the AEMs of the mgr class only.

On the other hand, when the right input is signaled at an AEM of class mgr, the token is forwarded to all AEMs of both classes since the matching object can be either a simple employee or a manager. The information about such a wide distribution is not stored at the right input class but at the left input class. This means that the signaled right input token is forwarded to the AOP of class emp and the latter is responsible for distributing it to its own AEMs and to the AOPs of all its direct subclasses. Then, each AEM that receives the token performs exactly the same action; distributes the token locally and forwards it to its own direct subclasses. This process continues until all the AEMs of the whole class hierarchy beneath the emp class receive the right input token.

Finally, consider the following example of an inter-object pattern that consists of three intra-object patterns. For the sake of simplicity, we assume that classes are not connectable through the class hierarchy.

```
IF  A@a(attr₁:X,attr₂:Y)  and  B@b(attr₃:Y,attr₄:Z)  and
    C@c(attr₅:Z,attr₆:W)
THEN  <action>
```

When the intra-object event for class A is signaled, it is forwarded to the left input of the A−B inter-object event. The token is then propagated to the right input of this inter-object event at class B. Finally, the signaled tokens are forwarded to the left input of the next inter-object event. Since the left input of the second inter-object event is the first inter-object event, it is distributed to all the AOPs that the first inter-object event is distributed into, namely classes A and B. Therefore, this example shows that the left input and memory of an inter-object event can be distributed to two or more classes, depending on how many intra-object events are joined to produce an inter-object event.

The right input and memory of any inter-object event is always stored at one AOP since the join is always performed on a left-to-right strategy. When the right input of the second inter-object event is signaled, the token is propagated to all the AEMs of both A and B classes since the left memory of this event is distributed across the AEMs of both classes. This distribution scheme is embedded inside the event definition so that the right input can directly forward the tokens for join at the appropriate processors.

The deletion of tokens is efficiently performed by means of deletion optimization (see chapter 4). Negative tokens are deleted from the corresponding memory without joining them with memories stored at different AEMs, unless the negative token is received by the last events of the network. In the above example, assume that a negative token is signaled at the left input of the A–B inter-object event which is located at an AEM of class A. The token is matched and deleted from the local left memory and forwarded to the left memory of the second inter-object event. The latter is distributed to both A and B classes, as explained above; therefore, the negative token is distributed to AEMs of both classes to be matched and deleted.

Finally, since the second inter-object event is the last of the network, deletion optimization does not hold and the negative token is joined with tokens of the right memory at the AEMs of class C. If the negative token was originated from class C, instead, the token should be distributed to all AEMs of classes A and B because the left memory is stored in these two classes.

The matching algorithms for negative two-input events are pretty much the same with the ones we have presented for the positives ones. However, we notice that, in some cases, double joins between the positive and negative inputs of the negative event are required (see chapter 4). The double joins impose, of course, extra communication between the AEMs of the two (or more classes) involved in the negative event and its inputs.

Parallel Rule Execution

In the previous subsection it was mentioned that each AEM at each AOP has a local rule manager which receives fired rule instantiations from the local event manager. If rules were distributed in such a way so that the action part updated only the local database, then each local rule manager could run its own rules independently from the rest of the rule managers. However, such a rule distribution may be difficult to achieve. Furthermore, rules that their actions affect multiple AEMs and AOPs are more expressible.

When a rule affects many sites, then rule managers must be synchronized at some point of rule execution. This is vital for the correctness of the global computation. We have already extensively referred to rule interference and serializability as a correctness criterion in the previous chapter. Furthermore, rule ordering due to priorities or other rule evaluation control strategies may impose that certain rules should run before others. If these rules reside at different sites, then these sites must communicate at run-time to decide how to distributely run a set of rules so that their result is serializable, i.e. equivalent to a sequential execution with a correct order.

PRACTIC^{KB} follows mainly the locking paradigm for concurrent rule execution [118]. However, as pointed out by Ceri and Widom [34], a simple locking scheme does not suffice when the database is distributed, as it is in a shared-nothing parallel machine, and when rule execution among the multiple sites is asynchronous. However, the PRACTIC^{KB} system avoids the conservative table-level locking scheme of Ceri and Widom by providing special locks used only by the rule evaluation algorithm.

In the sequel, we assume that rules are partially ordered using some ordering scheme that assigns an integer number to each rule. The smallest the number, the higher priority the rule has. Such a rule ordering scheme may emulate all rule ordering schemes, provided that there is a mapping between the rule ordering scheme and the domain of integers. For example, rule ordering based on a rule graph [136] can be transformed into an integer mapping by using topological ordering.

The ordering of each rule type will be discussed at the corresponding paragraph. We begin the presentation of parallel rule execution using production and deductive rules. Then we conclude with active rules which provide a variety of rule execution times.

Production rules. The ordering of production rules can be either directly imposed by rule priority numbers or by the heuristic conflict resolution criteria usually used for production rules. For example, as we described in chapter 4, rule specificity can be directly mapped onto an integer indicating the complexity of the discrimination network for the rule condition. This number can be used to provide a partial rule ordering scheme for production rules. Recency could also be used but it requires extensive run-time communication and clock synchronization among the processors. Therefore, we have chosen to use recency only inside the local rule manager.

Another assumption we use for parallel rule execution is that all sites begin processing rules in a synchronized fashion. When the global transaction issues an end of transaction message or even a rule checkpoint message, this is distributed to all associated AOPs and AEMs and the local rule managers begin their rule processing cycles. Ceri and Widom have presented a locking scheme for asynchronous start of rule processing [34]. However, their scheme inhibits parallelism by locking entire tables. Furthermore, when an inconsistency is detected the rollback of rule processing at all sites is required and rule processing restarts synchronized. Thus, we believe that there is a little benefit on starting rule execution asynchronously.

On the other hand, local rule managers process their rules asynchronously after the synchronous start. This means that each rule manager may proceed at its own pace; it does not have to wait for other rule managers to execute exactly the same steps in the rule processing cycle. Of course, such an asynchronous execution requires certain synchronization actions in certain points, otherwise rule execution can become incorrect.

In Figure 23, the main loop for the rule processing cycle at each local rule manager is presented. The main point of our rule priority mechanism is that before a rule is executed, it first checks to see if other processors are about to execute rules. The processors with the highest priority rules are allowed to start execution while the rest must wait until the higher priority rules are executed. After that, the rule processors must assure that no other processor will execute a higher priority rule while they execute the currently selected one. This is done by requesting a rule priority lock from all processors (Figure 24).

If some of the processors are currently executing higher priority rules, then the nodes that have requested rule priority locks wait until the first ones are finished. Meanwhile, they watch out for database updates induced by remote action executions that might invalidate the current rule selection either by changing the condition elements of the rule or by inserting a higher priority rule at the conflict set.

If all processors grant the rule priority lock request, then the processor requests read and write locks for the objects referenced by the rule. The locking scheme has been described in the previous chapter. If locks are not granted, then again the selected rule may be invalidated. When the locks are granted, the rule can be safely executed.

This rule processing loop continues until the local conflict set gets empty and all the other participating rule processors respond positively about the emptiness of their local conflict sets as well. If at least one other processor has a non-empty conflict set, then the loop continues for all processors (Figure 25).

---

1. Include remote influence (Call `include_remote`)
2. IF `false` is returned THEN terminate the main loop ELSE continue
3. Manage the rule priority lock (Call `priority_lock`)
4. Pick-up the first rule from the ordered local conflict set (CS), so that its priority number LB is equal to or greater than the priority of the current rule priority lock
5. Let LP be a list with all processors except the local one
6. IF there are messages from other processors regarding priorities
    THEN collect all priority-processor pairs into list RP and go to 7
    ELSE request lock of rule priority (Call `priority_request(LP)`); Go to 1
7. If the first rule in RP has priority RB and RB<LB then the remote rule should be executed first; The local rule manager acknowledges this only to the processor of rule RB
8. If RB>LB then the local rule should be executed first; Call `priority_request(LP)`
9. If RB=LB then the remote rule and the local rule can be executed together;
    For all rules in RP with priority equal to LB the local rule manager acknowledges to their processors that they can run in parallel; Call `priority_request(LP)`
10. Loop back to step 1

Figure 23. Main loop of rule execution at each local rule manager

---

Procedure `priority_lock`
1. IF a lock release and a lock grant is input THEN release the first lock and grant the second one; Acknowledge
2. IF a single lock request is input THEN replace it with the new one. Acknowledge. (*the new one is less than or equal to the current one - otherwise it would have not been selected*)
3. IF a single lock release is input but the lock is not present (*already replaced*) THEN ignore it

Procedure `priority_request(list_of_processors)`
1. Let *n* be the length of `list_of_processors`
2. Try to acquire a rule priority lock from each processor in `list_of_processors`
3. Wait for *n* acknowledgments
4. IF *k<n* priority locks can be acquired (at once)
   THEN let `rest_of_processors` stand for the non-lock-granting processors.
           Call `remote_disable`.
   ELSE call `execute_rule`.
5. IF `false` is returned THEN call `priority_release` and return
   ELSE call `priority_request(rest_of_processors)`

Procedure `priority_release`
1. For all i<n processors that rule priority lock requests have been sent, send priority lock releases

Figure 24. Auxiliary procedures for rule priority lock management

---

Deductive rules. The ordering of deductive rules with negation is imposed by stratification which assigns an integer number, called stratum, to each derived class and its derivation rules. Thus, a partial ordering of deductive rules using priorities can be established.

Actually, deductive rules do not need the locking mechanism of production rules to maintain their correctness. The rule ordering imposed by stratification alone suffices to guarantee that rules do not interfere incorrectly. As explained in the previous chapter, rule interference can destroy serializability only when there are cyclic rule read-write interferences. However, stratification disallows such cyclic interferences by ordering the evaluation of derived classes so that classes that are negatively referenced by the derivation rule of another class are evaluated before (see chapter 2).

Thus, the parallel production rule execution algorithm is also used for deductive rules, with the exception that read/write rule locks are not requested in the procedure `execute_rule` in Figure 25 which now consists only of line 4.

Procedure include_remote
1. Wait for remote messages
2. IF the only message is a termination_request THEN
   IF the local CS is empty
   THEN respond true and wait for terminate message
        IF a terminate message is received THEN return true ELSE return false
   ELSE respond false
3. IF there is a termination_request message and data modification messages THEN respond false to the former and continue
4. IF there are data modification messages THEN include data modifications from remote sites to the local database; Propagate data modifications through the discrimination network and modify the local CS
5. IF the CS is empty THEN send a termination_request message to all *n* processors ELSE return true
6. Wait for responds
7. IF at least one false respond is received THEN return true
8. IF all responds are true THEN return false

Procedure remote_disable
1. Call include_remote
2. Call priority_lock
3. IF current rule instantiation is disabled THEN return false
4. IF a rule with higher priority is now at the CS THEN put the rule instantiation back to the local CS and return false
5. Return true

Procedure execute_rule
1. Try to acquire the correct read and write locks for the current rule instantiation
2. IF the locks cannot be acquired (at once) THEN call remote_disable ELSE go to 4
3. IF false is returned THEN return ELSE go to 1
4. Execute the rule action (by propagating the actions to remote processors)
5. Release read/write locks

Figure 25. Auxiliary procedures for parallel rule processing

One important issue regarding deductive rules is the location of the derived objects and the maintenance of the consistency of the materialized derived data. Derived classes are also handled as demon objects in PRACTIC^{KB}. This means that their instances are distributed to several AOPs. The distribution is based on the derived rules for a certain derived class; the rule graph that derives a certain class (including multiple rules) is analyzed and the base classes are collected. The derived class is then hosted by all AEMs of all those base class AOPs. The derived class, as an object, is stored at the master processor of APRAM. Queries regarding a derived class are forwarded (through the derived class definition at the master processor) to all the AOPs that host its instances.

When a deductive rule is fired, in much the same way with a production rule, then a derived object must be inserted in the database. In a centralized environment, as in the case of sequential DEVICE (see chapter 4), the database is checked for already existing objects with exactly the same attribute values. This is important for maintaining the consistency of materialized data through a counter mechanism.

In PRACTIC^{KB}, we have chosen to relax the global uniqueness of derived objects by just checking at the local database. This means, of course, that at remote rule processors the same object must already exist. However, we omit this check for performance reasons and we show that it does not jeopardize consistency. Consider the following deductive rule:

```
IF  A@a(attr₁:X,attr₂:Y) and B@b(attr₃:Y,attr₄:Z)
THEN c(attr₅:X,attr₆:Z)
```

Assume that: a) A and B are base classes, b) the AOP of class A already contains the object $a(attr_1:1,attr_2:1)$, and c) the AOP of class B already contains the object $b(attr_3:2,attr_4:3)$. If object $b(attr_3:1,attr_4:3)$ is created, it is joined with objects of class A and the derived object $c(attr_5:1,attr_6:3)$ must be created. The latter is stored at the AOP of class A.

Then, object $a(attr_1:1,attr_2:2)$ is created, joined with class B, and derived object $c(attr_5:1,attr_6:3)$ must be created and stored at the AOP of class B. However, this object already exists at the AOP of class A; therefore, duplicate derived objects exist at different processors. This inconsistency is allowed since it cannot lead to false derivations as we shall show.

First of all, direct updates of derived objects from the users are not allowed. Therefore, the existence of multiple copies does not jeopardize database consistency. Second, when a query is issued against a derived class and the answer contains duplicate objects, these are merged to a single one. Last but not least, is the maintenance of derived objects when base objects are modified.

In the above example, if object $a(attr_1:1,attr_2:2)$ is deleted then this deletion must be propagated through the deductive rule, and the derived object $c(attr_5:1,attr_6:3)$ must be deleted. Since the rule condition has only one inter-object event there is a join between class A and class B to find out which object should be deleted. Therefore, the derived object is deleted from class B because it is the last one that received a negative input signal.

The above derived object still exists in class A, though. In a centralized environment this would also be true because the object would have its counter set to 2 since it has two derivations. The deletion message would just decrease the counter by 1 and the object would still exist. However, in the parallel environment the behavior is different. For example, consider that the derived class C is referenced by another deductive rule:

IF C@c(attr$_5$:X,attr$_6$:Y) THEN d(attr$_7$:X,attr$_8$:Y)

The deletion of one of the copies of the derived object c(attr$_5$:1,attr$_6$:3) would cause the propagation of this deletion to the above rule. In the centralized environment this would not happen because the object is not deleted. This difference in behavior may cause consistency problems. However, if we examine the above example closer, we see that the propagation of the deletion of the derived object of class C will cause the deletion of an object of class D. However, the existence of two copies of the certain object means that there must exist two corresponding objects of class D as well. The two copies reside wherever the copies for the class C object reside. Thus the deletion of one of the copies of the class C object causes the deletion of one copy of the class D object.

In the centralized environment there would be only one copy for the class D object because only one class C object would exist with its counter set to 2. When the class C object is deleted, its counter is decreased and the deletion is not propagated. Thus at the end one object of both classes C and D would exist with their counters set to 1. This is exactly the same result with the parallel execution of PRACTIC^{KB}.

A more difficult case is when class C is used in a rule condition joined with another class, either base or derived. In the following example, class Q is a base class.

IF C@c(attr$_5$:X,attr$_6$:Z) and Q@q(attr$_9$:Z,attr$_{10}$:Y)
THEN d(attr$_7$:X,attr$_8$:Y)

Assume the previous case where two copies of a derived object for class C exist: one at class A and one at class B. Furthermore, this derived object matches with the object q(attr$_9$:3,attr$_{10}$:5). Therefore, two copies for the derived object d(attr$_7$:X,attr$_8$:Y) must exist. The location of these copies depends on the way the original join between classes C and Q was performed. If a left-to-right order is assumed, then there is only one copy of the above derived object of class D with its counter set to 2, located at the AOP of class Q. With a right-to-left join order two copies exist: one at each of A and B classes.

If object q(attr$_9$:3,attr$_{10}$:5) is deleted, the corresponding negative token is joined with class C at both AOPs of class A and B. If the second of the above joining scenarios is true, then both copies of the derived D class object will be correctly deleted. In the centralized environment there would be just one copy which should be deleted as well.

If the first joining scenario is true then the propagation of the deletion would require the deletion of two copies of the derived D class object at classes A and B. However, these copies do not exist! Instead one copy with its counter set to 2 is stored at class Q.

This inconsistency is resolved by requiring the following. When a derived object should be deleted but a copy of it does not exist at the local database then a deletion message is forwarded to all the classes involved in the condition of the rule that caused the deletion propagation. At this second level of deletion, when a class receives a deletion message but it cannot delete the requested object, it simply ignores the message. When a class receives multiple deletion messages it must try to react to all of them. Thus, if it has a copy of a derived object with its counter set to 2 and receives two messages, it must eventually delete the object. If the counter is less than the number of received messages, the un-serviced messages are ignored.

The above scheme works for any number of joined classes in the condition but we omit the presentation because it is more difficult to follow.

Active rules. The ordering of active rules is usually done through priorities. However, in some systems, such as EXACT [56] and OSAM/KB [136], the ordering is imposed by a rule graph that is defined by specifying for a rule which other rules precede it. However, as we have discussed at the beginning of this subsection, a rule graph can be also turned into a set of rules with priority numbers assigned to each rule.

Active rules cannot be handled in a uniform way, such as production and deductive rules, because there are many different dimensions of active rule semantics [113]. Specifically, ECA rules consist of three different entities that each one of them may be considered at a different time relative to the database updates and the transaction. Events can be raised before or after method invocation, conditions can be checked immediately after the triggering event or at the end of transaction, and actions can be executed immediately after the condition is checked or at the end of transaction. Furthermore, net effects of events can be considered or not. Finally, questions, such as how many rules relative to a triggering event should be executed and under which order, complicate things further.

Several of the above questions have not yet been answered for sequential, centralized active database systems; therefore, the exact notion of correctness does not exist for ECA rules. In order to keep our system simple, we will initially exclude certain combinations from the above alternative semantics and we will give simple solutions for the remaining ones. Specifically, we consider only the 4 ECA rule types shown in Table 1.

Event relative to method	EC coupling	CA coupling
before	immediate	immediate
after	immediate	immediate
after	immediate	deferred
after	deferred	immediate

Table 1. ECA rule types handled by PRACTIC[KB]

In addition to Table 1, we focus on ECA rules where the net effect of events is not considered because we assume that production rules already play that role. The absence of net effects makes the problem of parallel rule execution a lot easier because a triggered rule is going to fire even if its triggering event has been made obsolete by a subsequent update. Thus, a locking mechanism for the event of a rule is not required.

Another assumption that makes the problem easier is that triggering events are simple and that they consider a single object. Complex events can be tackled by production rules. Furthermore, we consider methods sent to single objects, rather than sets of objects. Finally, when multiple rules are triggered by the same event, there are two alternatives for how many rules should be executed: either a single one or all of them [56].

After the above assumptions are made, the problem of executing ECA rules in parallel is greatly simplified. In the following, we discuss parallel rule processing for each of the rule types of Table 1.

Immediate execution. The first two rule types in Table 1 are handled in the same way. Since each update triggers just one object and the ECA rule must react to this event immediately, we have chosen not to consider the effects of other rules triggered on other processors. The conflict set for immediate rules is localized to the AEM that the object resides and no priorities between rules of different rule processors are considered. Furthermore, the triggering events of the two immediate rule types are signaled at different points in time; therefore, these rule types are considered separately. However, there is rule ordering among the rules of the same type.

Each local rule processor forms the local conflict set relative to an update and a rule type. Following the rule ordering criteria, it picks up one rule for execution. Before the rule is scheduled for execution, read/write locks are requested. The condition and action of an ECA rule may involve remote objects; therefore, if a rule cannot acquire its locks, it must be suspended until the locks are released. The condition of ECA rules is evaluated in parallel, based on the hierarchical query execution algorithms of PRACTIC presented earlier in the chapter. The action is also executed in parallel on the objects selected by the condition.

If the rule scheduling policy suggests that only one rule should be fired, then the rest of the rules in the local conflict set are dropped and control returns to the transaction. Otherwise, the next rule is considered based on rule ordering. When there are no more rules left in the conflict set, control is also returned to the transaction. Nested rule triggering is supported by the immediate mode: if rule action triggers another rule, then the current rule processing phase is suspended and a new rule processing phase, relative to the new triggers, commences execution.

The third rule type of Table 1 is interesting because it combines both immediate and deferred execution. Specifically, rule condition evaluation is performed immediately after the event is triggered while action execution is deferred until the end of the transaction. Such a rule execution semantics, although awkward, exists for centralized active database systems. However, it must be expected that either the objects matched in the condition immediately after the event detection are not changed until the end of the transaction or that the action does not care for the values matched at the condition when the end of transaction is reached.

If any of these assumptions does not hold, then the action may try to modify objects while the object values (or even the objects) to be changed do not exist. The solution is to acquire read locks on the objects referred by the condition and to hold them until the action is executed. Read locks are released if the condition is not verified. If another rule of the same type tries to acquire read locks on the same objects, these are granted since read locks are shared. The action execution will be described below.

Deferred execution. The last rule type and the action execution phase of the third rule type of Table 1 are executed at the end of the transaction. Here, we remind that rule processing starts synchronously at each AEM when the global transaction is committed or at user-defined checkpoints but each local rule manager proceeds asynchronously, at its own pace.

The hybrid immediate-deferred rule type is executed by acquiring write locks on the objects to be changed in the action. This may require changing the read locks to write locks when an object is referred to in the condition and modified in the action. If write locks cannot be acquired then the local rule manager must wait until locks held by other processors are released.

Priorities of rules triggered on different processors are not considered for hybrid rules. This may be justified by the fact that rule processing really begins immediately after the simple event is detected and read locks are acquired at that time. There is no point in ordering rules that acquire read locks only at that point because locks can be shared and there is no rule interference.

In addition, there is no point in ordering the action execution order at the end of the transaction because rules cannot interfere with each other; read locks for conditions have already been acquired, conditions have already been verified, and rule interference cannot take place. Here, we suppose that actions consist only of data modifications and do not read data themselves. Several active database systems, such as STARBURST [145], allow reading data in the action but this mainly happens because these systems do not have a mechanism for passing data from the condition to the action.

The rules of the purely deferred rule type (rule type 4 in Table 1) are executed in much the same way as production rules. The only difference with production rules is that the net effect of events is not considered. This is reflected by eliminating line 3 from procedure `remote_disable` in Figure 25. The rest of the main loop and auxiliary procedures remain the same.

Here, we must notice that the execution of actions for deferred rules may trigger additional rules that belong to any of the four types of Table 1. However, at the end of transaction there is no distinction between immediate and deferred coupling modes. Therefore, the four rule types of Table 1 degenerate to two, namely the ones triggered before and after method execution.

In EXACT [56], each different rule type models a different ECA rule application, such as integrity constraints, derived data, etc.; therefore, the ordering between these rule types is defined by the application programmer or the database administrator. The rules within each rule type are considered in isolation with the rest of the rule types and possibly following a strict ordering. In addition to rule type ordering, there is a rule ordering inside each rule type. Therefore, each rule type has its own conflict set.

In PRACTIC^{KB}, instead of maintaining four different conflict sets, we isolate rule types by multiplying the priority of each rule by a factor that indicates the priority of the rule type. For example, the most prioritized rule type has a factor of 1, the next rule type has a factor of e.g. 100 and so on and so forth. Thus, all rules can be in the same conflict set and the correct order among rule types is maintained.

8 CONCLUSIONS AND FUTURE DIRECTIONS

In this chapter, we summarize the material we have presented throughout the book. The book consists of two parts. The first part is concerned with Knowledge Base Management Systems (KBMS), i.e. database management systems extended with rule facilities. We have presented how relational and object-oriented database (OODB) systems have been extended with either deductive or active rules. We have analyzed various implementation techniques, giving special emphasis on those parts of the implementation that can be re-used in order to hook in the database system multiple rule types, if possible.

In the sequel, we have presented various techniques that integrate multiple rule types into the same database system. The integration has been achieved either by unifying the semantics of rule types, such as production and deductive rules, or by emulating the operational semantics of one another. In the latter case, there are approaches both for integrating events and event-driven rules into a production or deductive rule system and for emulating declarative rules into an event-driven environment.

We have, finally, described in detail the DEVICE system which integrates multiple declarative rule types into an active OODB that supports only the lowest-level event-driven rules. The result of such an integration is a flexible, yet efficient, KBMS that allows the user to work with many rule types, according to the application type and/or his/her programming proficiency level.

More specifically, the highest the rule level type, the more naive programmer the user can be. For example, deductive rules are used for declaratively specifying complex views, i.e. queries to the data, production rules are used for programming in an expert system style and enforcing integrity constraints, whereas ECA rules can be used for a variety of data maintenance, security, and integrity enforcement tasks, including programming applications.

One of the great challenges of such systems is to foresee, analyze, and resolve the interactions among the various rule types and users that program them. For example, rules enforced by database administrators must reside centrally in the database server, while user-defined applications would run locally, at the client site. Conflicts, priority policies, and rule interaction techniques must be further researched.

Of course, the most important aspect of engineering such complex and loosely coupled systems is the correct rule analysis and design. The above interactions could be avoided at an early stage of application development, if tools that foresee the interactions and their consequences are at the hand of the database administrator or the application developer.

Finally, user-friendly programming tools that facilitate the development and debugging of applications written using such rule languages should be developed. Moreover, tools that generate rules from even higher specifications, such as visual programming languages and/or very high-level textual descriptions, would give a boost to the limited usability of rules in current commercial products.

In the second part of the book we have presented research issues and techniques employed for parallel database and knowledge base systems. The former have interesting techniques for parallelizing and speeding-up user queries and database operations. Since the core of every knowledge base is a database, the techniques used for parallel databases are a guideline for defining the useful and acceptable techniques for knowledge bases.

Parallel knowledge bases are mainly concerned with matching and executing multiple rules in parallel. The concurrent execution of multiple rules may lead to inconsistency problems arising when two contradicting rules are executed at the same time. One of the criteria used for identifying the correctness of both parallel database and knowledge base systems is the equivalence of execution with sequential systems. Serializability of execution is achieved either by analyzing the interactions between rules or by locking the data that a rule operates upon. Parallel execution techniques for all rule types have been discussed.

At the end of the second part of the book we have presented a parallel knowledge base system, named PRACTIC^{KB}, which tries to preserve the sequential semantics of rule programming on a parallel hardware. The core of the system is a parallel object-oriented database system, named PRACTIC. PRACTIC employs hierarchical query execution strategies to exploit the hierarchical nature of OODB organization. The rule integration scheme of DEVICE is mapped onto the parallel model of PRACTIC, and rules are matched and executed in parallel and in an asynchronous way. The resulting system is a knowledge base system that is as flexible as DEVICE but only more efficient.

The adherence of parallel knowledge base systems to sequentiality has two faces. Programmers and users do not have to worry about learning how to program in parallel. They still program sequentially; however, their programs run faster in parallel. On the other hand, the potentials of parallel execution are not fully exploitable by sequential programming.

The practice with parallel systems, in general, has shown that they were anything but great commercial success stories. This is usually due to the price of such systems and the difficulty in programming them. Computer programmers with a parallel programming background are scarce and software engineering in terms of parallelism is even more complex than usual. Therefore, application customers tend to avoid parallelism because the software is hard to find, hard to develop, and hard to maintain.

On the other hand, parallel database systems are a very successful story. Many commercial products and applications are in the market for quite a few years now and the numbers tend to grow. This is due to the fact that these products do not offer parallelism but speed. End-users are not concerned with the fact that what they are dealing with is a parallel database server but a fast server. Database application programmers do not have to worry about special parallelism programming constructs either.

This transparency is achieved by the system by giving exactly the same functionality as a sequential database system. The rest of the transformations and optimizations are automatically performed by the system. In this way most of the old applications can still run on the new parallel system (possibly with insignificant modifications) but only faster.

The same attitude should be followed by the knowledge base community if they want their systems to be broadly accepted and not have the end of many parallel systems enterprises. Many researchers argued that the multiprocessor hardware offers so many new opportunities and alternatives for the programmer that sticking to the sequential semantics of rule languages would not exploit this great potential. This is understandable and the authors of this book greatly support it. However, the practice, again, has shown that new semantics for programming languages are not so easily absorbed by the programmers.

Perhaps the story of parallel database systems shows that, at least for the current decade, language semantics should remain mainly sequential. The underlying system would probably has to be "intelligent" enough to uncover the parallelism inherent in the sequential programs and execute it as efficiently as possible. The users would use their old rule languages to develop applications. Of course, if a user is competent enough to comprehend the new parallel programming constructs, then the system must be able to give him/her the possibility to use them. The only problem with the latter is that the system will not be able to help and optimize the program which will be in a quite lower level of description.

When the programming community is mature for the transition from the current programming era to the parallel programming era because all the available resources for improvement of current technology have been exhausted, then perhaps new parallel programming languages (including parallel rule languages), combined with knowledge on how to engineer parallel software, will dominate. Even then, current techniques for optimizing sequential constructs on parallel hardware will provide a valuable technology to build on.

It is expected that in the near future fast computer networks, working in parallel for a problem, will compete with parallel computer systems, mainly because they are inexpensive. This homomorphism, along with the increasing speed of widely distributed networks, will lead to the unification of parallel and distributed systems. We believe that parallel computers will persist and that the competition will turn into cooperation by having networks of small parallel computers instead of a single, large parallel computer.

The current trend in parallel and distributed knowledge base systems is to develop large scale knowledge-based applications in order to overcome the difficulties in developing intelligent software. We believe that the next decade will establish knowledge-based applications into the main-stream of software technology since the demanding complexity of modern real-world problems requires the use of human expertise to be dealt with.

A distinctive feature that knowledge base systems must have for future applications is activeness. Active knowledge base systems will respond intelligently to emerging situations without user intervention. Knowledge-based systems that are built on such a reactive behavior will be able to control complex distributed systems in a seamless manner.

As an example of a distributed, reactive knowledge-based application we mention a distributed expert system, that the authors are currently working on, that will manage a TCP-IP based national level WAN in an intelligent manner. Another example is the use of an active knowledge base system for defining and maintaining the consistency of complex views in a data warehouse [19]. In both of these systems a distributed version of PRACTIC^{KB} is used.

APPENDIX
The Declarative Rule Language Syntax of DEVICE

```
<production_rule> ::=
    if <condition> then <action>
<deductive_rule> ::=
    if <condition> then <derived_class_template>
<derived_attribute_rule> ::=
    if <condition> then <derived_attribute_template>
<condition> ::=
    <inter-object-pattern>
<inter-object-pattern> ::=
    <condition-element> ['and' <inter-object-pattern>]
<inter-object-pattern> ::=
    <inter-object-pattern> 'and' <prolog_cond>
<condition-element> ::=
    ['not'] <intra-object-pattern>
<intra-object-pattern> ::=
    [<var>'@']<class>['('<attr-patterns>')']
<attr-patterns> ::=
    <attr-pattern>[','<attr-patterns>]
<attr-pattern> ::=
    <var-assignment> | <predicate>
<attr-pattern> ::=
    <attr-function>':'<var> <rel-operator> <value>
<var-assignment> ::=
    <attr-function>':'<var>
<predicate> ::=
    <attr-function> <predicates>
```

```
<predicates> ::=
      <rel-operator> <value> [{ & | ; } <predicates>]
<rel-operator> ::=
      = | > | >= | =< | < | \=
<value> ::=
      <constant> | <var>
<attr-function> ::=
      [<attr-function>'.']<attribute>
<prolog_cond> ::=
      'prolog' '{'<prolog_goal>'}'
<action> ::=
      <prolog_goal>
<derived_class_template> ::=
      <derived_class>'('<templ-patterns>')'
<derived_attribute_template> ::=
      <var>'@'{<class>}'('<templ-patterns>')'
<templ-patterns> ::=
      <templ-pattern> [',' <templ-pattern>]
<templ-pattern> ::=
      <attribute>':'{<value> | <aggr_func>'('<var>')'}
<aggr_func> ::=
      count | sum | avg | max | min
<class> ::=
```
An existing OODB class or derived class
```
<derived_class> ::=
```
An existing OODB derived class or a non-existing OODB class
```
<attribute> ::=
```
An existing attribute of the corresponding OODB class or derived class
```
<prolog_goal> ::=
```
An arbitrary Prolog/ADAM goal
```
<constant> ::=
```
A valid constant of an OODB simple attribute type
```
<var> ::=
```
A valid Prolog variable

References

[1]   S. Abiteboul and A. Bonner, Objects and views, *ACM SIGMOD Int. Conf. on the Management of Data*, 1991, pp. 238-247.

[2]   S. Abiteboul and S. Grumbach, COL: A logic-based language for complex objects, *Int. Conf. on Extending Database Technology*, 1988, pp. 271-293.

[3]   S. Abiteboul and P.C. Kanellakis, Object identity as a query language primitive, *ACM SIGMOD Int. Conf. on the Management of Data*, 1989, pp. 159-173.

[4]   A. Acharya, M. Tambe, and A. Gupta, Implementation of production systems on message-passing computers, *IEEE Trans. on Parallel and Distributed Systems*, 3(4), pp. 477-487, 1992.

[5]   G. Agha, Concurrent object-oriented programming, *Communications of the ACM*, 33(9), pp. 125-141, 1990.

[6]   R. Agrawal and H.V. Jagadish, Multiprocessor transitive closure algorithms, *Int. Symposium on Databases in Parallel and Distributed Systems*, Austin, Texas, USA, 1988, pp. 56-66.

[7]   P. America, POOL-T: A parallel object-oriented language, in *Object-Oriented Concurrent Programming*, A. Yonezawa and M. Tokoro, Eds.: MIT Press, 1987.

[8]   P. Apers, C. Berg, J. Flokstra, P. Grefen, M. Kersten, and A. Wilschut, PRISMA/DB: A parallel, main memory relational DBMS, *IEEE Trans. on Knowledge and Data Engineering*, 4(6), pp. 541-554, 1992.

[9]   M.P. Atkinson, F. Bancilhon, D.J. DeWitt, K.R. Dittrich, D. Maier, and S.B. Zdonik, The object-oriented database system manifesto, *Int. Conf. on Deductive and Object-Oriented Databases*, Kyoto, Japan, 1989, pp. 223-240.

[10] E. Bahr, F. Barachini, J. Doppelbauer, H. Grabner, F. Kasparec, T. Mandl, and H. Mistelberger, A parallel production system architecture, *Journal of Parallel and Distributed Computing*, 13, pp. 456-462, 1991.

[11] N. Bassiliades and P.M.D. Gray, CoLan: A functional constraint language and its implementation, *Data & Knowledge Engineering*, 14(3), pp. 203-249, 1995.

[12] N. Bassiliades and I. Vlahavas, Modelling constraints with exceptions in object-oriented databases, *International Conference on the Entity-Relationship Approach*, Manchester, U.K., 1994, pp. 189-204.

[13] N. Bassiliades and I. Vlahavas, A non-uniform data fragmentation strategy for parallel main-memory database systems, *Int. Conf. on Very Large Databases*, Zurich, Switzerland, 1995, pp. 370-381.

[14] N. Bassiliades and I. Vlahavas, PRACTIC: A concurrent object data model for a parallel object-oriented database system, *Information Sciences*, 86(1-3), pp. 149-178, 1995.

[15] N. Bassiliades and I. Vlahavas, Hierarchical query execution in a parallel object-oriented database system, *Parallel Computing*, 22(7), pp. 1017-1048, 1996.

[16] N. Bassiliades and I. Vlahavas, DEVICE: Compiling production rules into event-driven rules using complex events, *Information and Software Technology*, 39(5), pp. 331-342, 1997.

[17] N. Bassiliades and I. Vlahavas, Processing production rules in DEVICE, an active knowledge base system, *Data & Knowledge Engineering*, 24(2), pp. 117-155, 1997.

[18] N. Bassiliades, I. Vlahavas, and A. Elmagarmid, E-DEVICE: An extensible knowledge base system with multiple rule support, Dept. of Computer Science, Purdue University, W. Lafayette, Indiana, Technical Report, CSD-TR #97-048, October 1997.

[19] N. Bassiliades, I. Vlahavas, A.K. Elmagarmid, and E.N. Houstis, InterBase[KB]: A knowledge-based multidatabase system for data warehousing, Dept. of Computer Science, Purdue University, W. Lafayette, Indiana, Technical Report, CSD-TR #97-047, October 1997.

[20] D.A. Bell, J. Shao, and M.E.C. Hull, A pipelined strategy for processing recursive queries in parallel, *Data & Knowledge Engineering*, **6**, pp. 367-391, 1991.

[21] B. Bergsten, M. Couprie, and P. Valduriez, Overview of parallel architectures for databases, *The Computer Journal*, **36**(8), pp. 734-740, 1993.

[22] M. Berndtsson and B. Lings, On developing reactive object-oriented databases, *IEEE Data Engineering Bulletin*, **15**(4), pp. 31-34, 1992.

[23] L. Bic and R.L. Hartmann, AGM: A dataflow database machine, *ACM Trans. on Database Systems*, **14**(1), pp. 114-146, 1989.

[24] H. Boral, W. Alexander, L. Clay, G. Copeland, S. Danforth, M. Franklin, B. Hart, M. Smith, and P. Valduriez, Prototyping Bubba, a highly parallel database system, *IEEE Trans. on Knowledge and Data Engineering*, **2**(1), pp. 4-24, 1990.

[25] H. Boral and D.J. DeWitt, Database machines: an idea whose time has passed? A critique of the future of the database systems, *Int. Workshopon Database Machines*, Munich, Germany, 1983.

[26] H. Branding, A.P. Buchmann, T. Kudrass, and J. Zimmermann, Rules in an open system: The REACH rule system, *Int. Workshop on Rules in Database Systems*, Edinburgh, Scotland, 1993, pp. 111-126.

[27] D.A. Brant and D.P. Miranker, Index support for rule activation, *ACM SIGMOD Int. Conf. on the Management of Data*, 1993, pp. 42-48.

[28] W. Bronnenberg, L. Nijman, E. Odijk, and R. Twist, "DOOM: a decentralized object-oriented machine," in *IEEE Micro Machine*, 1987, pp. 52-69.

[29] P.L. Butler, J.D. Allen, and D.W. Bouldin, Parallel architecture for OPS5, *Int. Symp. on Computer Architecture*, Honolulu, Hawaii, 1988, pp. 452-459.

[30] F. Cacace, S. Ceri, S. Crespi-Reghizzi, L. Tanca, and R. Zicari, Integrating object-oriented data modelling with a rule-based programming paradigm, *ACM SIGMOD Int. Conf. on the Management of Data*, 1990, pp. 225-236.

[31] F. Cacace, S. Ceri, and M.A.W. Houtsma, A survey of parallel execution strategies for transitive closure and logic programs, *Distributed and Parallel Databases*, **1**(4), pp. 337-382, 1993.

[32] M.J. Carey, D.J. DeWitt, M. Franklin, N.E. Hall, M.L. McAuliffe, J.F. Naughton, D.T. Schuh, M.H. Solomon, C. Tan, O.G. Tsatalos, S.J. White, and M.J. Zwilling, Shoring up persistent applications, *ACM SIGMOD Int. Conf. on the Management of Data*, Minneapolis, USA, 1994, pp. 383-394.

[33] S. Ceri, G. Gottlob, and L. Tanca, *Logic Programming and Databases*. Berlin: Springer-Verlag, 1990.

[34] S. Ceri and J. Widom, Production rules in parallel and distributed database environments, *Int. Conf. on Very Large Databases*, Vancouver, Canada, 1992, pp. 339-351.

[35] S. Ceri and J. Widom, Deriving incremental production rules for deductive data, *Information Systems*, **19**(6), pp. 467-490, 1994.

[36] S. Chakravarthy, E. Anwar, L. Maugis, and D. Mishra, Design of Sentinel: An object-oriented DBMS with event-based rules, *Information and Software Technology*, **39**(9), pp. 555-568, 1994.

[37] S. Chakravarthy and D. Mishra, Snoop: An expressive event specification language for active databases, *Data & Knowledge Engineering*, **14**(1), pp. 1-26, 1994.

[38] J.-P. Cheiney and C.d. Maindreville, A parallel strategy for transitive closure using double hash-based clustering, *Int. Conf. on Very Large Databases*, Brisbane, Australia, 1990, pp. 347-358.

[39] W. Chen and D.S. Warren, C-logic of complex objects, *ACM SIGACT-SIGMOD-SIGART Symposium on Principles of Database Systems*, 1989, pp. 369-378.

[40] D. Chimenti, R. Gamboa, R. Krishnamurthy, S. Naqvi, S. Tsur, and C. Zaniolo, The LDL system prototype, *IEEE Trans. on Knowledge and Data Engineering*, **2**(1), pp. 76-90, 1990.

[41] C. Collet, T. Coupaye, and T. Svensen, NAOS - Efficient and modular reactive capabilities in an object-oriented database system, *Int. Conf. on Very Large Databases*, Santiago, Chile, 1994, pp. 132-143.

[42] T.A.-N. Consortium, The active database management system manifesto: A rulebase of ADBMS features, *SIGMOD Record*, **25**(3), pp. 40-49, 1996.

[43] G. Copeland, W. Alexander, E. Boughter, and T. Keller, Data placement in Bubba, *ACM SIGMOD Int. Conf. on the Management of Data*, Chicago, USA, 1988, pp. 99-108.

[44] T. Corporation, DBC/1012 data base computer system manual, Doc. No. C10-0001-02, Release 2.0, Novermber 1985.

[45] C.J. Date, *Introduction to Database Systems*, vol. Volume I, 6th Edition ed: Addison-Wesley, 1995.

[46] U. Dayal, A.P. Buchman, and D.R. McCarthy, The HiPAC project, in *Active Database Systems: Triggers and Rules for Advanced Database Processing*, J. Widom and S. Ceri, Eds.: Morgan Kaufmann Publishers, 1996, pp. 177-206.

[47] L.M.L. Delcambre and J. Etheredge, The Relational Production Language: A production language for relational databases, *Int. Conf. on Expert Database Systems*, Vienna, Virginia, 1988, pp. 333-351.

[48] M.A. Derr, S. Mocrishita, and G. Phipps, The Glue-Nail deductive database system: Design, implementation, *The VLDB Journal*, **3**(2), pp. 123-160, 1994.

[49] H.M. Dewan, D. Ohsie, S.J. Stolfo, O. Wolfson, and S.D. Silva, Incremental database rule processing in PARADISER, *Journal of Intelligent Information Systems*, **1**(2), pp. 177-209, 1992.

[50] D. DeWitt, S. Ghandeharizadeh, D.A. Schneider, A. Bricker, H. Hsiao, and R. Rasmussen, The GAMMA database machine project, *IEEE Trans. on Knowledge and Data Engineering*, **2**(1), pp. 44-62, 1990.

[51] D. DeWitt and J. Gray, Parallel database systems: The future of high performance database systems, *Communications of the ACM*, **35**(6), pp. 85-98, 1992.

[52] D.J. DeWitt and R.H. Gerber, Multiprocessor hash-based join algorithms, *Int. Conf. on Very Large Databases*, Stockholm, Sweden, 1985, pp. 151-164.

[53] D.J. DeWitt, D.F. Lieuwen, and M. Mehta, Pointer-based join techniques for object-oriented databases, *Int. Conf. on Parallel and Distributed Information Systems*, San Diego, CA, USA, 1993, pp. 172-181.

[54] D.J. DeWitt, J. Naughton, and J. Burger, Nested loops revisited, *Int. Conf. on Parallel and Distributed Information Systems*, San Diego, CA, 1993, pp. 230-242.

[55] D.J. DeWitt, J.F. Naughton, J.C. Shafer, and S. Venkataraman, ParSets for parallelising OODBMS traversals: Implementation and performance, *The VLDB Journal*, **5**(1), pp. 3-18, 1996.

[56] O. Diaz and A. Jaime, EXACT: An extensible approach to active object-oriented databases, Dept. of Languages and Information Systems, University of the Basque Country, San Sebastian, Spain 1994.

[57] O. Diaz, N. Paton, and P.M.D. Gray, Rule management in object oriented databases: A uniform approach, *Int. Conf. on Very Large Databases*, Barcelona, Spain, 1991, pp. 317-326.

[58] A.A.A. Fernandes, N.W.Paton, M.H. Williams, and A. Bowles, Approaches to deductive object-oriented databases, *Information and Software Technology*, **34**(12), pp. 787-803, 1992.

[59] C.L. Forgy, OPS5 user manual, Dept. of Computer Science, Carnegie-Mellon University 1981.

[60] C.L. Forgy, RETE: A fast algorithm for the many pattern/many object pattern match problem, *Artificial Intelligence*, **19**, pp. 17-37, 1982.

[61] S. Ganguly, A. Silberschatz, and S. Tsur, A framework for the parallel processing of datalog queries, *ACM SIGMOD Int. Conf. on the Management of Data*, Atlantic City, New Jersey, USA, 1990, pp. 143-152.

[62] H. Garcia-Mollina and K. Salem, Main memory database systems: An overview, *IEEE Trans. on Knowledge and Data Engineering*, **4**(6), pp. 509-516, 1992.

[63] S. Gatziu and K.R. Dittrich, Events in an active object-oriented database, *Int. Workshop on Rules in Database Systems*, Edinburgh, Scotland, 1993, pp. 23-39.

[64] S. Gatziu, A. Geppert, and K.R. Dittrich, Integrating active concepts into an object-oriented database system, *Workshop on Database Programming Languages*, Nafplion, Greece, 1991, pp. 399-415.

[65] J.-L. Gaudiot and A. Sohn, Data-driven parallel production systems, *IEEE Trans. on Software Engineering*, **16**(3), pp. 281-293, 1990.

[66] N.H. Gehani and H.V. Jagadish, Active database facilities in ODE, in *Active Database Systems: Triggers and Rules for Advanced Database Processing*, J. Widom and S. Ceri, Eds.: Morgan Kaufmann Publishers, 1996, pp. 177-206.

[67] N.H. Gehani, H.V. Jagadish, and O. Shmueli, Event specification in an active object-oriented database, *ACM SIGMOD Int. Conf. on the Management of Data*, 1992, pp. 81-90.

[68] A.v. Gelder, A message passing framework for logical query evaluation, *ACM SIGMOD Int. Conf. on the Management of Data*, Washington, D.C., USA, 1986, pp. 155-165.

[69] A. Goldberg and D. Robson, *Smalltalk-80, The Language and its Implementation*: Addison-Wesley, 1983.

[70] G. Graefe, Volcano, An extensible and parallel dataflow query processing system, *IEEE Trans. on Knowledge and Data Engineering*, **6**(1), pp. 120-135, 1994.

[71] P.M.D. Gray, K.G. Kulkarni, and N.W. Paton, *Object-Oriented Databases, A Semantic Data Model Approach*. London: Prentice Hall, 1992.

[72] U. Griefahn and R. Manthey, Update propagation in Chimera, an active DOOD language, *Int. Workshop on the Deductive Approach to Information Systems and Databases*, Spain, 1994, pp. 277-298.

[73] A.S. Grimshaw, Easy-to-use object-oriented parallel processing with Mentat, *IEEE Computer*, **26**(5), pp. 39-51, 1993.

[74] T.P. Group, A benchmark of non-stop SQL on the debit-credit transaction, *ACM SIGMOD Int. Conf. on the Management of Data*, Chicago, IL, 1988, pp. 337-341.

[75] A. Gupta, *Parallelism in Production Systems*. Los Altos, California: Morgan-Kaufman, 1987.

[76] A. Gupta, I.S. Mumick, and V.S. Subrahmanian, Maintaining views incrementally, *ACM SIGMOD Int. Conf. on the Management of Data*, 1993, pp. 157-166.

[77] E.N. Hanson, Gator: A generalized discrimination network for production database rule matching, *IJCAI Workshop on Production Systems and their Innovative Applications*, 1993.

[78] E.N. Hanson, The Ariel project, in *Active Database Systems: Triggers and Rules for Advanced Database Processing*, J. Widom and S. Ceri, Eds.: Morgan Kaufmann Publishers, 1996, pp. 177-206.

[79] E.N. Hanson and J. Widom, An overview of production rules in database systems, *The Knowledge Engineering Review*, 8(2), pp. 121-143, 1993.

[80] J.V. Harrison and S.W. Dietrich, Integrating active and deductive rules, *Int. Workshop on Rules in Database Systems*, Edinburgh, Scotland, 1993, pp. 288-305.

[81] M.A.W. Houtsma, P.M.G. Apers, and S. Ceri, Distributed transitive closure computations: The disconnection set approach, *Int. Conf. on Very Large Databases*, Brisbane, Australia, 1990, pp. 335-346.

[82] M.A.W. Houtsma, A.N. Wilschut, and J. Flokstra, Implementation and performance evaluation of a parallel transitive closure algorithm on PRISMA/DB, *Int. Conf. on Very Large Databases*, Dublin, Ireland, 1993, pp. 206-217.

[83] D. Hsiao, *Advanced Database Machine Architectures*: Prentice Hall, 1983.

[84] I.-M. Hsu, M. Singhal, and M.T. Liu, Distributed rule processing in active databases, *IEEE Int. Conf. on Data Engineering*, Tempe, Arizona, USA, 1992, pp. 106-113.

[85] S.P. Hufnagel and J.C. Browne, Performance properties of vertically partitioned object-oriented systems, *IEEE Trans. on Software Engineering*, 15(8), pp. 935-946, 1989.

[86] G. Hulin, Parallel processing of recursive queries in distributed architectures, *Int. Conf. on Very Large Databases*, Amsterdam, The Netherlands, 1989, pp. 87-96.

[87] T. Ishida, Parallel firing of production system programs, *IEEE Trans. on Knowledge and Data Engineering*, 3(1), pp. 11-17, 1991.

[88] T. Ishida and S. Stolfo, Toward parallel execution of rules in production system programs, *Int. Conf. on Parallel Processing*, 1985, pp. 568-575.

[89] Z. Jiao and P.M.D. Gray, Optimization of methods in a navigational query language, *Int. Conf. on Deductive and Object-Oriented Databases*, Munich, Germany, 1991, pp. 22-42.

[90] M.A. Kelly and R.E. Seviora, A multiprocessor architecture for production system matching, *AAAI Nat'l Conf. on Artificial Intelligence*, Seattle, Washington, 1987, pp. 36-41.

[91] J. Kiernan, C.d. Maindreville, and E. Simon, Making deductive databases a practical technology: A step forward, *ACM SIGMOD Int. Conf. on the Management of Data*, Atlantic City, NJ, 1990, pp. 237-246.

[92] M. Kifer and G. Lausen, F-logic: a higher-order language for reasoning about objects, inheritance, and scheme, *ACM SIGMOD Int. Conf. on the Management of Data*, 1989, pp. 134-146.

[93] M. Kifer and J. Wu, A logic for object-oriented programming (Maier's O-Logic revisited), *ACM SIGACT-SIGMOD-SIGART Symposium on Principles of Database Systems*, 1989, pp. 379-393.

[94]   K. Kim, Parallelism in object-oriented query processing, *IEEE Int. Conf. on Data Engineering*, 1990, pp. 209-217.

[95]   W. Kim, *Introduction to Object-Oriented Databases*: MIT Press, 1990.

[96]   M. Kitsuregawa and Y. Ogawa, Bucket spreading parallel hash: A new, robust, parallel hash join method for data skew in the Super Database Computer (SDC), *Int. Conf. on Very Large Databases*, Brisbane, Australia, 1990, pp. 210-221.

[97]   W. Klas, K. Aberer, and E. Neuhold, Object-oriented modelling for hypermedia systems using the VODAK model language, in *Object-Oriented Database Management Systems, NATO ASI Series*. Berlin: Springer-Verlag, 1993.

[98]   C.-M. Kuo, D.P. Miranker, and J.C. Browne, On the performance of the CREL system, *Journal of Parallel and Distributed Computing*, 13(4), pp. 424-441, 1991.

[99]   S. Kuo and D. Moldovan, Implementation of multiple rule firing production systems on hypercube, *AAAI Nat'l Conf. on Artificial Intelligence*, Anaheim, CA, USA, 1991, pp. 304-309.

[100] C.d. Maindreville and E. Simon, A production rule based approach to deductive databases, *IEEE Int. Conf. on Data Engineering*, 1988, pp. 234-241.

[101] F.G. McGabe, *Logic and Objects*: Prentice Hall, 1992.

[102] J. Minker, *Foundations of Deductive Databases and Logic Programming*, Los Altos: Morgan Kaufmann, 1988.

[103] D.P. Miranker, TREAT: A better match algorithm for AI production systems, *AAAI*, 1987, pp. 42-47.

[104] D. Moldovan, RUBIC: A multiprocessor for rule-based systems, *IEEE Trans. on Systems, Man, and Cybernetics*, 19(4), pp. 699-706, 1989.

[105] D. Neiman, Control issues in parallel rule-firing production systems, *AAAI Nat'l Conf. on Artificial Intelligence*, 1991, pp. 310-316.

[106] K. Oflazer, Partitioning in parallel processing of production systems, PhD dissertation, Dept. of Computer Science, Carnegie-Mellon University, Pittsburgh, Pennsylvania, 1986.

[107] P. O'Neil, *Database Principles, Programming, Performance*: Morgan Kaufmann, 1994.

[108] A.O. Oshisanwo and P.P. Dasiewicz, A parallel model and architecture for production systems, *Int. Conf. on Parallel Processing*, 1987, pp. 147-153.

[109] N.W. Paton, ADAM: An object-oriented database system implemented in Prolog, *British National Conf. on Databases*, 1989, pp. 147-161.

[110] N.W. Paton, Supporting production rules using ECA rules in an object-oriented context, *Information and Software Technology*, 37(12), pp. 691-699, 1995.

[111] N.W. Paton and O. Diaz, Object-oriented databases and frame-based systems: a comparison, *Information and Software Technology*, 33(5), pp. 357-365, 1991.

[112] N.W. Paton, O. Diaz, and M.L. Barja, Combining active rules and meta-classes for enhanced extensibility in object-oriented systems, *Data & Knowledge Engineering*, 10, pp. 45-63, 1993.

[113] N.W. Paton, O. Diaz, M.H. Williams, J. Campin, A. Dinn, and A. Jaime, Dimensions of active behaviour, *Int. Workshop on Rules in Database Systems*, Edinburgh, Scotland, 1993, pp. 40-57.

[114] N.W. Paton and P.M.D. Gray, Optimising and executing Daplex queries using Prolog, *The Computer Journal*, 33(6), pp. 547-555, 1990.

[115] S. Potamianos and M. Stonebraker, The POSTGRES rule system, in *Active Database Systems: Triggers and Rules for Advanced Database Processing*, J. Widom and S. Ceri, Eds.: Morgan Kaufmann Publishers, 1996, pp. 177-206.

[116] R. Ramakrishnan, D. Srivastava, S. Sudarshan, and P. Seshadri, The CORAL deductive system, *The VLDB Journal*, **3**(2), pp. 161-210, 1994.

[117] L. Raschid, T. Sellis, and A. Delis, A simulation-based study on the concurrent execution of rules in a database environment, *Journal of Parallel and Distributed Computing*, **20**(1), pp. 20-42, 1994.

[118] L. Raschid, T.K. Sellis, and C.-C. Lin, Exploiting concurrency in a DBMS implementation for production systems, *Int. Symp. on Databases in Parallel and Distributed Systems*, Austin, Texas, USA, 1988, pp. 34-45.

[119] L. Raschid and S.Y.W. Su, A parallel processing strategy for evaluating recursive queries, *Int. Conf. on Very Large Databases*, Kyoto, Japan, 1986, pp. 412-419.

[120] M. Richeldi and J. Tan, JazzMatch: Fine-grained parallel matching for large rule sets, *IEEE Int. Conf. on Data Engineering*, Vienna, Austria, 1993, pp. 616-623.

[121] T. Risch and M. Skold, Active rules based on object-oriented queries, *IEEE Data Engineering Bulletin*, **15**(4), pp. 27-30, 1992.

[122] J.G. Schmolze, Guaranteeing serializable results in synchronous parallel production systems, *Journal of Parallel and Distributed Computing*, **13**(4), pp. 348-365, 1991.

[123] J.G. Schmolze and S. Goel, A parallel asynchronous distributed production system, *AAAI Nat'l Conf. on Artificial Intelligence*, Boston, MA, USA, 1990, pp. 65-71.

[124] D.A. Schneider and D.J. DeWitt, A performance evaluation of four parallel join algorithms in a shared-nothing multiprocessor environment, Portland, Oregon, 1989, pp. 110-121.

[125] M.H. Scholl, C. Laasch, and M. Tresch, Updatable views in object-oriented databases, *Int. Conf. on Deductive and Object-Oriented Databases*, Munich, Germany, 1991, pp. 189-207.

[126] T. Sellis, C.-C. Lin, and L. Raschild, Coupling production systems and database systems: A homogeneous approach, *IEEE Trans. on Knowledge and Data Engineering*, **5**(2), pp. 240-255, 1993.

[127] E. Simon and J. Kiernan, The A-RDL System, in *Active Database Systems: Triggers and Rules for Advanced Database Processing*, J. Widom and S. Ceri, Eds.: Morgan Kaufmann Publishers, 1996, pp. 111-149.

[128] E. Simon, J. Kiernan, and C.d. Maindreville, Implementing high level active rules on top of a relational DBMS, *Int. Conf. on Very Large Databases*, Vancouver, Canada, 1992, pp. 315-326.

[129] M. Skold and T. Risch, Using partial differencing for efficient monitoring of deferred complex rule conditions, *IEEE Int. Conf. on Data Engineering*, 1996, pp. 392-401.

[130] J. Srivastava, K.-W. Hwang, and J.S.E. Tan, Parallelism in database production systems, *IEEE Int. Conf. on Data Engineering*, Los Angeles, California, USA, 1990, pp. 121-128.

[131] M. Stefik and D. Bobrow, Object-oriented programming: Themes and variations, *AI Magazine*, **6**(4), pp. 40-62, 1986.

[132] S. Stolfo, D.P. Miranker, and R. Mills, A simple processing scheme to extract and load balance implicit parallelism in the concurrent match of production rules, *AFIPS Symp. Fifth Generation Computing*, 1985.

[133] S. Stolfo, O. Wolfson, P. Chan, H. Dewan, L. Woodbury, J. Glazier, and D. Ohsie, PARULEL: Parallel rule processing using meta-rules for redaction, *Journal of Parallel and Distributed Computing*, **13**, pp. 366-382, 1991.

[134] S.J. Stolfo, Five parallel algorithms for production system execution on the DADO machine, *AAAI Nat'l Conf. on Artificial Intelligence*, Austin, Texas, 1984, pp. 300-307.

[135] M. Stonebraker, R. Katz, D. Patterson, and J. Ousterhout, The design of XPRS, *Int. Conf. on Very Large Databases*, Los Angeles, CA, 1988, pp. 318-330.

[136] S.Y.W. Su, R. Jawadi, P. Cherukuri, Q. Li, and R. Nartey, OSAM*.KBMS/P: A parallel, active, object-oriented knowledge base server, Dept. of Computer and Information Sciences, University of Florida, Gainesville, Technical Report TR94-031, 1994.

[137] A.K. Thakore, S.Y.W. Su, and H. Lam, Algorithms for asynchronous parallel processing of object-oriented databases, *IEEE Trans. on Knowledge and Data Engineering*, 7(3), pp. 487-504, 1995.

[138] J. Ullman, *Principles of Database and Knowledge-Base Systems*. Rockville, Maryland: Computer Science Press, 1989.

[139] J. Ullman, A comparison between deductive and object-oriented database systems, *Int. Conf. on Deductive and Object-Oriented Databases*, Munich, 1991, pp. 263-277.

[140] J. Vaghani, K. Ramamohanarao, D.B. Kemp, Z. Somogyi, P.J. Stuckey, T.S. Leask, and J. Harland, The Aditi deductive database system, *The VLDB Journal*, 3(2), pp. 245-288, 1994.

[141] P. Valduriez, Parallel database systems: Open problems and new issues, *Distributed and Parallel Databases*, 1(2), pp. 137-165, 1993.

[142] P. Valduriez and S. Khoshafian, Parallel evaluation of the transitive closure of a database relation, *Int. Journal of Parallel Programming*, 17(1), 1988.

[143] S. Venkatarman, M. Livny, and J. Naughton, Impact of data placement on memory management for multi-server OODBMS, *IEEE Int. Conf. on Data Engineering*, Taipei, Taiwan, 1995, pp. 355-364.

[144] J. Widom, Deductive and active databases: Two paradigms or ends of a spectrum?, *Int. Workshop on Rules in Database Systems*, Edinburgh, Scotland, 1993, pp. 306-315.

[145] J. Widom, The Starburst rule system, in *Active Database Systems: Triggers and Rules for Advanced Database Processing*, J. Widom and S. Ceri, Eds.: Morgan Kaufmann Publishers, 1996, pp. 177-206.

[146] J. Widom and S. Ceri, *Active Database Systems: Triggers and Rules for Advanced Database Processing*: Morgan Kaufmann Publishers, 1996.

[147] A.N. Wilschut, J. Flokstra, and P.M.G. Apers, Parallelism in a main-memory DBMS: The performance of PRISMA/DB, *Int. Conf. on Very Large Databases*, Vancouver, Canada, 1992, pp. 521-532.

[148] J.L. Wolf, D.M. Dias, and P.S. Yu, An effective algorithm for parallelizing sort merge in the presence of data skew, *Int. Symposium on Databases in Parallel and Distributed Systems*, Dublin, Ireland, 1990, pp. 103-115.

[149] O. Wolfson, H.M. Dewan, S.J. Stolofo, and Y. Yemini, Incremental evaluation of rules and its relationship to parallelism, *ACM SIGMOD Int. Conf. on the Management of Data*, Denver, Colorado, USA, 1991, pp. 78-87.

[150] O. Wolfson and A. Ozeri, A new paradigm for parallel and distributed rule-processing, *ACM SIGMOD Int. Conf. on the Management of Data*, Atlantic City, New Jersey, USA, 1990, pp. 133-142.

[151] C. Zaniolo, Object identity and inheritance in deductive databases - An evolutionary approach, *Int. Conf. on Deductive and Object-Oriented Databases*, Kyoto, Japan, 1989, pp. 7-21.

[152] C. Zaniolo, A unified semantics for active and deductive databases, *Int. Workshop on Rules in Database Systems*, Edinburgh, Scotland, 1993, pp. 271-287.

Index

Active class, 105
Active database manifesto, 23
Active database system, 3; 13; 20; 37; 130
Active Extension Manager (AEM), 109
Active knowledge base system, 37; 102
Active object, 106
Active Object Processor (AOP), 108
Active rule, 3; 14; 20; 101; 120; 130
ADAM system, 8; 39; 106
Ad-hoc query, 6; 81; 110
Adornment, 17; 46
Aggregate attribute, 58
AGM system, 79
AMOS system, 31
A-RDL system, 22; 30
ARIEL system, 22; 25; 29; 87
Asynchronous execution, 95
Atomic formula, 15
A-TREAT network, 25
Attribute pattern, 39

Base data, 15
Blocking approach, 86
Bottom-up evaluation, 16; 28; 97

Checkpoint, 22; 29; 43; 132
CHIMERA system, 31
Class extension, 9
Class partition, 112
Class-hierarchy parallelism, 79; 111
Compilation process, 54
Complex attribute, 8; 40; 81
Complex event, 22; 32; 46
Complex event network, 32; 42; 46; 57
Complex object, 8; 81
Compound event. see Complex event
Condition element, 24; 31; 57
Conflict resolution criteria, 24; 35; 58; 96; 124
Conflict set, 24; 31; 42; 58; 85; 92; 125
Consequent, 39
Context, 95
Convergence, 95

Copy-and-constrain method, 86
Coupling modes, 23; 34; 133
CREL system, 92; 95

DADO system, 86
Data availability, 67; 72
Data consistency, 68; 96; 128
Data definition language, 6
Data distribution, 69; 73; 86; 112
Data manipulation language, 6; 41; 64
Data parallelism, 69; 112; 115
Data partition, 68; 74; 112
Data placement, 75; 81
Data reduction, 86; 97
Data replication, 68; 73
Data skew, 69; 72; 115
Data type, 6; 8
Database schema, 6; 74; 80; 111
Data-driven rule. see Production rule
Data-flow, 85; 100
Datalog, 15; 27; 93
Datalog**, 97
DATEX system, 25
Deadlock, 68; 94
Deadlock detection, 68
Decision support query, 66; 69
Declarative rule, 2; 28
Decoupled execution, 23
Deductive database system, 13; 15; 45; 97
Deductive object-oriented database, 18
Deductive rule, 2; 15; 28; 31; 33; 41; 44; 96; 97; 126
Deferred execution, 23; 103; 132
Delete-and-re-derive method, 32
Delta relations, 29
Demon, 22
Demon object, 118; 127
Dependency graph, 16; 45; 89; 100
Dependency graph analysis, 89
Derived attribute, 58
Derived class template, 41
DEVICE system, 32; 37; 87; 105
DIPS system, 25; 93
Disconnection set approach, 100
Discrimination network, 24; 32; 46; 84; 120

Distributed-memory architecture. *see* Shared-everything architecture

ECA rule, 14; 20; 21; 28; 30; 102; 130
Encapsulation, 3; 7; 19; 112; 121
Event, 3; 21; 28; 102; 118
Event anti-signaling, 47
Event detection, 21; 45; 120; 132
Event manager, 21; 32; 42; 120
Event signaling, 21; 35; 42; 47; 120; 131
Event-driven rule. *see* ECA rule
EXACT system, 21; 39; 43; 130; 133
Expert database system, 83
Extensibility, 39; 58; 73
Extensional database (EDB), 15

Fixpoint, 17; 30; 43

Hash bucket, 70; 85
Hash join, 70; 121
Hash partitioning, 75
Hierarchical query execution, 115
Horizontal partitioning, 74; 112
Hybrid architecture, 73
Hybrid memory, 55

Immediate execution, 23; 103; 131
Incomplete token, 49
Incremental condition matching, 24; 33
Infinite derivations, 17
Inheritance, 9
Input token, 47
Intentional database (IDB), 15; 28
Inter-class parallelism, 111
Inter-object event, 48; 119
Inter-object parallelism, 112
Inter-object pattern, 39
Inter-operator parallelism, 69
Inter-transaction parallelism, 68; 75
Intra-class parallelism, 80; 109; 112
Intra-object event, 48; 119
Intra-object parallelism, 110
Intra-object pattern, 39; 46
Intra-transaction parallelism, 69

Join, 7; 56; 70
Join optimization, 56

Keys, 6
Knowledge, 1; 13
Knowledge acquisition, 1
Knowledge base, 2
Knowledge base management system, 2; 13; 27
Knowledge base system, 2; 13; 37; 83; 105
Knowledge engineer, 1
Knowledge-based systems, 1

LEAPS algorithm, 25
Linear recursive rule, 100
Locking, 67; 93; 101; 109; 123; 131
Locking protocol, 67; 93
Logical event, 48; 57; 119

Magic predicates, 17
Magic sets, 17; 46
Means-Ends-Analysis, 92
Message, 7
Message recipient, 7
Meta-rule, 92
Method, 7
Method body, 113
Method signature, 7
Mixin, 107
Multi-join query, 25; 70
Multi-rule approach, 31

Negation, 16; 51
Negative condition element, 51; 93
Negative event, 51; 123
Negative pattern, 40
Negative token, 42; 49; 123
Net effect, 35; 44; 130
Node parallelism, 79
Non-materialized deductive rule, 45
Non-passive object, 107
Non-uniform partitioning, 77

Object, 7; 78
Object attribute, 8; 47
Object-oriented database, 7; 18; 21; 37; 78; 105
Object-oriented knowledge base system, 37; 102; 105
ODE system, 22
OLTP, 66; 72; 80

On-line transaction processing. *see* OLTP
OPRA system, 31
OPS5, 1; 23; 39; 42; 87; 92
Optimization, 19; 46; 49; 54; 81; 123
OSAM system, 79; 102; 130
Output token, 47

PARADISER system, 93; 96; 99
Parallel condition matching, 84
Parallel database system, 63; 105
Parallel join execution, 70
Parallel knowledge base system, 83; 105
Parallel OODB system, 64; 78; 105
Parallel production system, 84
Parallel rule execution, 87; 123
Parallel rule matching, 120
PARS system, 96
Partitioning, 74; 97; 109
PARULEL system, 86; 92
Passive object, 107
Path parallelism, 79
Path query. *see* Transitive closure query
PF algorithm, 30
Pipelined parallelism, 70
Positive condition element, 93
Positive token, 42; 52
POSTGRES system, 22
PRACTIC system, 80; 105
PRACTIC^{KB} system, 94; 99; 102; 118
Primary copy, 68
Primitive event. *see* Simple event
PRISMA system, 64; 75; 100
Production cycle, 23; 43; 84; 95
Production memory, 23
Production rule, 2; 14; 20; 31; 32; 42; 84; 124; 131
Production system, 23; 32; 84; 87
Projection, 7
Prolog, 1; 15; 18; 39; 110

Query execution plan, 56; 70; 110
Query optimization, 19; 57
Query response time, 69

Range partitioning, 75
RDL1 system, 25; 27; 87
Read-write interference, 88
Recency, 43; 124
Recursive rule, 16; 98

Refractoriness, 43
Relation attribute, 6; 15; 74
Relational database, 6; 15; 22; 64
Relational operator, 7; 69
Relational table, 6; 25; 64
RETE network, 24; 48; 84
Round-robin partitioning, 74
RPL system, 25
RUBIC system, 91; 95
Rule action, 14; 20; 24; 40; 123; 133
Rule base, 2
Rule body, 15
Rule conclusion, 15; 41; 50; 96
Rule condition, 14; 20; 24; 28; 35; 39; 46; 84; 101
Rule execution control, 87; 95
Rule graph cycle, 16; 90
Rule head, 15; 28; 41
Rule instantiation, 24; 42; 86; 123
Rule interference, 88
Rule locking, 22; 101; 126
Rule maintenance, 34
Rule manager, 22; 33; 42; 58; 120
Rule priority locking, 125

Safe rule, 17
Scalability, 75
Scale-up, 65
Selection, 6; 17; 68; 110
Semi-active object, 107
Semi-naive evaluation, 16; 45; 98
Serializability, 67; 87; 99; 126
Set-oriented semantics, 15; 45; 64; 87
Shared-everything architecture, 71; 96
Shared-memory architecture. *see* Shared-everything architecture
Shared-nothing architecture, 72; 94; 96; 102; 108; 124
SHORE system, 80
Sideways information passing method, 17
Simple event, 22; 31; 42; 46; 119
Single-rule approach, 32
Situation-action rule, 14
Specificity, 43; 124
Speed-up, 65; 76; 100; 116
STARBURST system, 22; 31; 101; 133
Storage optimization, 55
Stratification, 16; 30; 45; 97; 126
Stratum, 17; 30; 99; 126

Synchronous execution, 95

Token, 25; 33; 42; 79; 84
Token deletion, 49
Token deletion optimization, 49; 123
Transaction, 22; 43; 66; 93; 101; 124
Transaction atomicity, 67
Transaction bandwidth, 67
Transaction committment, 29; 67; 94; 132
Transitive closure query, 100
TREAT network, 25; 86
Trigger, 22
Tuple, 6; 16; 24; 33; 42; 66; 74
Tuple marking method, 22
Tuple-oriented semantics, 87
Two-input event, 48; 119
Two-phase locking, 67; 93; 102

UMP-OPS5 system, 94
Uniform partitioning, 75

Vertical partition, 79
Vertical partitioning, 74
Virtual memory, 55

Working memory, 23; 84
Working memory element, 24; 84
Write-write interference, 89

XY-stratification, 30

α-memory, 24; 48; 85

β-memory, 24; 48; 85